MW01076256

RISE OF THE
ONE-WORLD
MIND

HOW TO THRIVE UNDER THE THREAT OF GLOBALISM

By Joshua R. Davis

All Scripture quotations are from the King James Version
of the Holy Bible unless otherwise indicated.

For more information, contact:
BEACON STREET PRESS
500 Beacon Drive
Oklahoma City, OK 73127
1-800-652-1144
www.swrc.com

Printed in the United States of America

ISBN 978-1-933641-95-9

DEDICATION

To the watchmen who have faithfully
sounded God's unchanging truths
amidst challenging times.

Thank you for staying on the wall!

CONTENTS

ACKNOWLEDGMENTS

Without the Lord Jesus, I can do nothing, thus my acknowledgments must begin with giving praise to Him. God's Word reveals the spirit of the last days and provides hope so that we can thrive. I pray this book draws many closer to Jesus.

I am beyond grateful for my family members who have supported me and encouraged me every step of the way. Thank you for your love and praycrs.

Thank you to my church family. I pray this book is a special blessing to each of you as you seek to know and grow in God's truth. Keep walking with Jesus!

To the incredible team at Southwest Radio Ministries, thank you is not enough. Countless hours of hard work and deep thought are invested into this project. I say a special thanks to each one who had a role in bringing this project to life including Matthew Hill, Lise Cutshaw, Edward Webber, Ginny Tallent, Shelly Morgan, Mary Massarueh, and Gary Bellamy.

I add a special thank you to Dr. Larry Spargimino for writing the foreword. You exemplify a true watchman on the wall! Thank you for your godly example and constant encouragement.

To God alone be the glory and praise for what He accomplishes through this project!

Maranatha!

FOREWORD

Tragically, and with epoch-making transformation, we are being sucked into a globalist, one-world way of thinking. The principle is most evident. Your mind matters. Proverbs 23:7 says that as a man "thinketh in his heart so is he." Expand that to – "as a culture thinketh in its heart so is the world."

Because this "one-world way of thinking" has become firmly entrenched in the minds of many through the media and the public school system, we find diminishing resistance to a bondage so onerous that no one will be able to extricate themself from it—unless their thinking changes.

Rise of the One-World Mind, by Joshua R. Davis will help the reader not be duped by an evil system that is leading to a demise of the values that made America great.

It has been correctly said that "a man convinced against his will is of the same opinion still." It is also true that "a man convinced with the assent of his own will, will gladly go along with virtually anything, no matter how grievous, painful and dangerous to his own well-being." This is exactly what is happening. The one-world way of thinking is like a chigger bite. The noxious substance first desensitizes the skin, and then, while the victim is totally unaware of it, the tiny mite slips in a poison which causes intense itching and misery.

The current mega-shift of values is evident to some. However, those of us who are aware of it look like conspiracy theorists and troublemakers to a large portion of society. Those with discernment know that there is a conspiracy, and it is not a theory. And, yes, we need to oppose it. The information in this volume will help the reader establish a degree of credibility with those who need to understand the dark forces that are at work in our world.

No doubt, this is a weighty topic and Josh Davis does not sugarcoat any of it. However, there is a refreshing, positive attitude that pervades the entire book. "I am convinced," writes the author, "we can live with peace instead of panic and confident hope instead of fearful anxiety."

Pastor Larry Spargimino, Ph.D.
Host of the Watchman On The Wall Broadcast of Southwest Radio Ministries

RISE OF THE
ONE-WORLD
MIND

HOW TO THRIVE UNDER THE THREAT OF GLOBALISM

INTRODUCTION

A threat is rising across our world. It will fundamentally transform every life on planet Earth. It is setting the stage for the biblical end-times scenario. The Antichrist and his cronies will utilize this system to its fullest extent imaginable. Our world is moving this way right now and most do not realize it is happening. This threat has a name – globalism.

"Wow! I had no clue these things were happening!" This is a common reaction I receive when I share how globalism is rising in our world. Admittedly, I was ignorant and unaware of many of these truths until recent years. The goal of this book is not to scare you into hiding in a cave but to open your eyes to the global transformation happening and to give you a roadmap for moving forward amid the rise of the one-world mind.

Distraction begets ignorance. Absorbed in our world filled with entertainment, games, events, and cat videos, we ignore the radical plans for global transformation quietly at work. You owe it to yourself, your family, and your community to wake up to the globalist agenda. Our response to this growing crisis will determine the kind of world the youngest among us will inherit. More than that, I pray this book impacts eternity for you or someone you love.

Quite frankly, I would have ignored a book like this a few years ago. I used to assume this kind of message was either a clever marketing ploy or a preacher's over-zealous affinity for breaking news mixed with an under-zealous affinity for God's Word. While a small handful of misguided preachers and downright charlatans may be guilty of those motivations, that is not my heart. As my eyes and ears opened to what was taking place in our world, I felt the burden of waking up the world.

God warned us to watch out for this end-times mindset in His Word, the Bible. Ignoring these truths is to our peril. But the news is not all bad. God gives us hope to guide us safely through this darkness.

That's why I devote several chapters of this book to explaining how we should move forward. I am convinced we can live with peace instead of panic and confident hope instead of fearful anxiety in today's uncertain world. We do not have to hunker down fearfully peeking through the blinds at the darkness outside our homes, praying just to survive this dark night. God can use us to change this world with His light.

Before we can go forward in God's power, we must know what we face. We must understand what globalism is and how it is working in our world today. Simply defined, globalism desires to bring the world together as one – one in our nationality, our money, our worship, our values, and our thinking. We inch toward globalism with each passing day. I will spell out how this is happening as this book unfolds.

Globalism grows with a hefty price tag: the removal of personal freedoms. A global, cashless monetary system, for example, promises greater ease of access and the ability to instantly use your funds anywhere in the world.

But what happens when there is a major crisis and the global government decides to restrict shopping to a certain radius around your house? "Impossible," you say. We are rapidly moving toward a central bank digital currency. I'll outline those details for you in a later chapter, but consider what happens when you couple that with the kinds of lockdowns several countries experienced during COVID in 2020. It's easy to see how this could happen, given the right conditions.

Thinking globally pervades our culture. Its message urges us to put the needs of the world ahead of our own. Thinking globally will eventually change every detail of our lives.

How are these changes happening? Manipulation of our minds is occurring on a global scale to convince us this is the way we should go. I know how crazy it sounds to make that claim. Let me show you how it works.

GLOBAL BRAINWASHING

Identity Under Attack

Identity discussions have escalated in recent years. In 2022, U.S. Senator Marsha Blackburn asked then-Supreme Court nominee Ketanji Brown Jackson a simple question, "Can you provide a definition for the word woman?" After repeating the question back to Senator Blackburn, Ketanji Brown Jackson replied with one word, "No."

We question the basic definitions of what it means to be a human. Instead of two biological sexes, male and female, our culture lists a growing list of over 100 gender identities.

This intensifying identity debate is not limited to a battle of the sexes. Globalists are using our cultural confusion to cause us to question who we are on a global scale.

I am American and have lived my whole life in America. I share that to say that while we will spend a lot of time talking about globalism, many of my examples are drawn from my American experiences and discuss how American freedoms could be swept away if the globalists get their way.

The chorus to Lee Greenwood's famous song "God Bless the U.S.A." begins, "And I'm proud to be an American." However, the globalists want us to think of America less and last. Preference is given to the global whole over individual nations. Any political candidate that promotes an America-first agenda will be demonized by the global elites.

This book will pull back the curtain on the push for globalism. We must open our eyes to what is happening in our world. The globalists are manipulating our global identity crisis to fit their vision for a one-world system.

Guilt Weaponized

Like gasoline fuels a car, guilt fuels global manipulation. Forgive me. I just went against the global climate change agenda by mentioning gasoline. (Oh yes, we will discuss the role climate change plays in the globalist agenda.) I should have said, "Like electricity fuels a car."

How is the push for electric vehicles marketed? By guilt. We are made to feel guilty for using gasoline and diesel to fuel our vehicles because we are destroying the planet. If we want to help the planet, then we need to go electric.

Guilt goes far beyond electric vehicles. We are repeatedly shamed into submission. Consider this example: Al Gore passionately linked climate change and border crises at the 2023 World Economic Forum. (Don't worry, we will talk more about the globalist World Economic Forum too.) He exclaimed, "Look at the xenophobia and political authoritarian trends that have come from just a few million refugees. What about a billion?! We would lose our capacity for self-governance on this world! We have to act!" We will come back to this quote momentarily, but notice how he used guilt messaging.

Gore used guilt to motivate change as he linked his outlandish climate alarmism with the refugee border crises taking place across the world. In his logic, if a nation wants to retain its ability to govern, it must fully open its borders. The crises of border security, government, and climate change are all linked together in globalist thinking. I will expose these links as the book unfolds.

Do you remember the messaging and the mandates during 2020? Guilt played a major role in the government's attempts to corral us, and it worked. Need I mention mask mandates? We were guilt-tripped into covering our faces everywhere we went.

Consider this use of guilt as an example of how it can be used to manipulate people. My mother navigated our church's daycare ministry through the maze of mandates. The state declared it an essential business, but the government would allow them to open only if masks were worn and everyone's temperature was checked before entering the facility. The government's attitude became "Either do it our way or close!"

The government declared our daycare ministry was essential while the church it is connected to was not. Some people felt guilty for going to church. We were shamed into silence as we were told, "How dare you risk the health of innocent people by opening the church doors! You are putting people at risk as you open your mouth to sing in church! Don't you care about the elderly and at-risk population? Stay home! Flatten the curve!"

The message of guilt shifted as the vaccine became available. We were promised we could get rid of the masks if we were fully vaccinated. Churches could reopen. Choirs could reconvene. Family reunions and vacations could come back on the calendar.

This usage of guilt reveals classic brainwashing techniques at work on a worldwide scale.

Brainwashing works by driving a message of shameful guilt to isolate and disorient the subject to his breaking point. Leniency is then offered as a gift so he begins to think his brainwashers have his best interests at heart.

We were guilted into staying behind locked doors away from our loved ones for months. We were told the vaccine was our ticket to reunite with our families and friends, guilt free, and just in time for Thanksgiving and Christmas (as long as everyone else was also vaccinated, of course).

Brainwashing will deprive a man of water until he passes his breaking point. Along the way, the captor constantly preaches a message of guilt, "You cannot have any water because you are bad." When the victim passes his breaking point, the brainwasher will step in with a glass of water. Now the thirsty man begins to think the brainwasher is his savior instead of his captor.

The captor has redefined "good" and "bad" for the victim. Good is what matches the captor's agenda. This new good may very well be the opposite of what is freeing, healthy, and in the best interests of the victim. However, the victim is so broken, that he realigns what he calls good with the captor's definition so that he can have more water.

Now that the victim has realigned his values with the captor, he is encouraged to release his guilt and embrace his new self, his new identity. Peace and harmony will exist as long as the victim continues to live according to the values of the captor.

While Al Gore certainly isn't alone in guilt messaging, let's see the brainwashing message inside the words he shared at the 2023 WEF. First, he used guilt and shame. "Look at the xenophobia and political authoritarian trends that have come from just a few million refugees. What about a billion?!" Then, he used fear to scare people into action. "We would lose our capacity for self-governance on this world! We have to act!"

He used classic brainwashing techniques on the world stage to scare us to get on board with his agenda. Names like "science deniers," "xenophobes," and "racists" are commonly thrown around to shame people into getting in line.

Are your eyes and ears opening? I got a cold chill when I first realized what was going on behind the message he shared.

Crises Create Brainwashing Opportunities

Wars, financial recessions, and global pandemics create opportunities to exploit fear and change behavior. Our news media conditions us to hear fear. When a crisis strikes, we are anxious to hear any new developments. We want someone to tell us what to do. In the heat of those moments, we become ripe for manipulation.

We are more willing to surrender our freedoms during crises. When we hand over our freedoms, we reveal what we truly value the most. Most of us value a sense of safety and security more than we do freedom.

You may disagree with that last statement but consider this. Why were people so willing to follow the COVID government mandates beyond the point where they no longer made sense? Let's return to the COVID crisis as an example of how crises create brainwashing opportunities.

As the months rolled on in 2020, we noticed double standards coming from our governmental leaders. Some governors told people to stay home and avoid travel during the summer months, yet pictures surfaced of them out of state on vacation with their families.

Some in power seized the opportunity the COVID crisis created, which gave them greater control over our lives. We willingly forked over our freedoms so that we could have a sense of safety and security that we were doing our part to "stop the spread." We followed along like sheep doing what our shepherd told us to do. The Antichrist will similarly lead this world.

If you canceled your 2020 vacation plans, you gave up your freedom to travel. If you stopped going to church in 2020 and never returned, you gave up your freedom to worship. I could go on, but you get the point. Most Americans willingly laid down their freedom because we valued safety and security more.

News media can play a leading role in restricting freedom. Emotional news gets greater ratings. They make big bucks by stirring up our emotions. They have leveraged fear against the American public and have withheld vital information from us to keep us tuned in.

Let's stick with our COVID example to illustrate this point. We were commanded to wear our masks. People got creative and made their own stylish ones. Then in early 2022, the Centers for Disease Control finally admitted cloth masks do not stop COVID.

Do you recall how the shot was sold by the media? First, the experts promised if we got the shot, we would not get COVID. After vaccinated people started getting COVID, they changed their message. They said we need to get the shot so we won't be hospitalized due to COVID. Then vaccinated people were hospitalized due to COVID, so they changed their story again. Then they promised us if we got the shot, we wouldn't die from COVID. Sadly, vaccinated people started dying from COVID. So, the messaging changed to promote endless booster shots.

Fear motivated this message from the very beginning. People willingly gave up their freedoms. We were told that we could not fly on a plane without a vaccine. Some colleges and universities said they would not admit students who were not fully vaccinated. Some businesses and entire job sectors refused to employ anyone who was not fully vaccinated. The message was heard loud and clear: either comply or go away.

Just as the brainwasher offers a "choice" to the victim to realign their values and receive the lenient gift, we were offered a "choice" to comply so that we could receive the lenient gift of access to travel, education, worship, and work.

The End-Times Mindset

The Bible describes an eerily similar mindset absorbing the world during what it calls the Great Tribulation period. I believe this future event will be a seven-year period that follows the rapture of the church. I will discuss why I believe the Bible teaches the Pretribulation rapture of the church in Chapter 8 as we understand how to move forward in today's world.

The book of Revelation outlines this seven-year period in great detail in chapters 6-18. Revelation 13 describes the reign of the unholy trinity – the Antichrist, Satan, and the False Prophet. This empire will usher in a one-world government, one-world economy, and one-world worship.

One of the best-known features of the end-times economy is the mark of the beast, which is described in Revelation 13:16-18. Anyone wishing to buy or sell anything must have this mark. The Antichrist will bring in this system by using the same techniques we saw at work during the pandemic and through the likes of Gore.

We are being conditioned to think with a globalist mindset. I used to wonder how people could fall for the one-world system during the Great Tribulation. Now we are waking up to how it will transpire. The world will be led down the primrose path to its doom.

Brainwashing in the Bible

Nebuchadnezzar led his Babylonian army in victory over Judah and the city of Jerusalem. Daniel and three of his friends were Jewish young men who were taken captive in this defeat. Because of their tremendous potential, they were brought back to Babylon to be trained to serve King Nebuchadnezzar (Dan. 1:1-4).

The mental transformation techniques used on them are similar to what we see happening in our world today. Let's explore how the Babylonians attempted to transform these Jewish captives.

First, they were removed from their homeland and their family. Where they were taken *to* is as important as where they were taken *from*. The Bible says they were brought into "the land of Shinar" (Dan. 1:2). This is the site where the Tower of Babel was constructed (Gen. 11:1-9). In this place, God was opposed and sin prevailed. It would be very difficult to live a righteous life in such a wicked place. The Jewish captives were brought under the care of a new parent figure named Ashpenaz (Dan. 1:3).

The Bible tells us next that they were taken to the land of Shinar when they were "children" (Dan. 1:3-4). The Hebrew word translated as "children" can mean anything from a newborn to a young adult. But based on historical evidence, it seems Daniel and his friends would have been about 14-15 years old.[1] These are crucial years of a young man's life. The choices he makes over the next few years can change the course of his entire life.

It has been wisely said, "Show me your friends and I'll show you your future." The voices we listen to are transforming what we think about and how we think. That's why the Bible strongly encourages us to guard our hearts. God also instructs parents to invest His truth into their kids. Daniel and his friends were removed from godly instruction and placed under this pagan influence to transform every detail of their lives.

---

1   Stephen R. Miller, Daniel, vol. 18, The New American Commentary (Nashville: Broadman & Holman Publishers, 1994), 60.

Secondly, they were taught the literature and language of the Babylonians (Dan. 1:4). Their education was transformed as they were required to learn the Akkadian language of Babylon. They wanted to change the worldview of these young men. The goal was to make them completely Babylonian, and they knew it started by changing how they thought.

How we think becomes what we believe. What we believe shapes our values. What we value shapes our behavior and our choices.

Why do you think there is such a battle in America over what our young people are taught in public schools and universities? If you can influence today's young minds, you can control the future. Globalists know this. That's why they are investing billions of dollars each year in education, media, and other programs to influence young minds with their agenda as early as possible.

Thirdly, their diet was changed to a Babylonian diet. King Nebuchadnezzar did not hold back the banquet. He commanded that they receive the same food he ate. Who wouldn't jump head-first into this bounty fit for a king?

For Daniel and his Hebrew friends, this new diet went further than food. It was an issue of obedience and allegiance. God had set down dietary laws in the best interests of His people.[2] Whom would they obey? Whom would they allow to determine "good" for them? Who would be their chief authority?

There is an intense battle raging in our culture over what is good. Young people who grew up in Christian homes have bought into what the world calls "good" and God calls "evil." This is the process of Romans 1:18-32 in action.

Fourthly, the Babylonians took their time with this transformation. They determined to train these young men for three years (Dan. 1:5). This wasn't like going to school. They couldn't go back home in the afternoon. This was 24/7 training so they would be ready to serve King Nebuchadnezzar. Changing thinking, values, beliefs, and behaviors takes time. The Babylonians invested that time to get the results they wanted.

What we see happening on a global scale today reveals a slow, steady trans-formation over a long time. Some of the agendas and mindsets I will show you go back almost 100 years. The globalists have their long-range goals in sight

---

2   It is outside the scope of this section to launch into a deep discussion on the Old Testament dietary laws. Some people question, "Why doesn't the church follow these dietary restrictions from the Old Testament?" Simply put, God specifically told Peter and others they had permission to eat foods that were once "off limits." See especially Mark 7:19; Acts 10; Romans 14.

and are slowly moving this world in their direction. COVID sped up the process and, in one sense, served as a litmus test for how our world will respond when another global crisis hits.

Fifthly, Daniel and his three friends were given Babylonian names (Dan. 1:6-7). Daniel became Belteshazzar. Hananiah became Shadrach. Mishael became Meshach. Azariah became Abednego. Without diving deep into the linguistics of the Hebrew and the Neo-Babylonian Akkadian languages, we can simply summarize the name change this way: each name moved the focus off of Israel's God and onto the pagan Babylonian deity.[3]

Their very identity was centered around Babylon and its gods. The goal was to change absolutely everything about them. Whom they worshiped would determine the outcome of this experiment. Would Daniel and his friends blindly follow the Babylonian attempts to radically transform their identity, thinking, behavior, life purpose, and destiny? Would they give into the brainwashing techniques employed on them?

Battling Brainwashing Biblically

The answer to these questions hinges on one verse. Daniel 1:8 says, "But Daniel purposed in his heart that he would not defile himself with the portion of the king's meat, nor with the wine which he drank: therefore he requested of the prince of the eunuchs that he might not defile himself."

Daniel chose God as his ultimate authority. He chose to honor God above anyone else as he refused the diet Babylon demanded. Daniel took a firm stand but he did so respectfully. How do we know that? First, verse 8 tells us, "he requested." He was in no position to make demands, yet he appealed nonetheless. Secondly, the next verse says, "Now God had brought Daniel into favour and tender love with the prince of the eunuchs" (Dan. 1:9).

We should take a bold stand against the brainwashing attempts of our day. However, the Christian army will shoot itself in the foot if we do not do so respectfully as Daniel did. His respectful attitude toward others opened the door for the test he proposed in the following verses.

---

3   For those who are curious about the linguistics behind these name changes, several commentaries are helpful. See, for example, Stephen R. Miller, *Daniel*, vol. 18, *The New American Commentary* (Nashville: Broadman & Holman Publishers, 1994), 65 and J. Dwight Pentecost, "Daniel," in *The Bible Knowledge Commentary: An Exposition of the Scriptures*, ed. J. F. Walvoord and R. B. Zuck, vol. 1 (Wheaton, IL: Victor Books, 1985), 1330. Both these men have slightly different opinions, which I find very helpful in weighing the evidence.

To summarize what happens in the following verses, Daniel proposed a ten-day test. He and his three friends would eat and drink their normal diet while others partook of the king's Babylonian banquet. After ten days, their health was measured and these four looked healthier than anyone else.

Guess what happened as a result? The Babylonians changed their minds. They instituted Daniel's diet for everyone in this training program (Dan. 1:16).

Please do not miss this point. When these four stood firmly on God's truth, they influenced their captors. In our day, our resolve could be tested. Will we stand on what we know is true or will we wilt in the face of pressure to conform?

What if Daniel and his friends had simply given in? Would we have this book of the Bible? Would we miss out on the tremendous truths this book contains?

Thank God they did not give in to the brainwashing pressure. As a result, God endowed them with greater intellectual ability, insight, and wisdom than all others.

They faced the biggest test of their entire training when they had to stand before the king. Would their strong stand be considered open rebellion against the ruler who conquered their country? Their lives could be on the line. You can breathe a sigh of relief because King Nebuchadnezzar declared them to be ten times wiser than all his other advisors (Dan. 1:17-20).

Instead of closing their eyes and going with the Babylonian system, these four opened the eyes of the Babylonians when they took their stand. Isn't that amazing? I pray that our stand today will open the eyes of others around us.

When you keep God as your ultimate authority, you will never regret it. These four men show us how to boldly, yet respectfully, stand up in the battle for truth. Because of their stand, our world has been blessed by them for thousands of years. Their fellow Jews who caved to the Babylonian brainwashing are forgotten. How could God use our biblical stand in this generation to transform others?

I placed the adjective "biblical" before "stand" on purpose. We can take a strong political stand against globalism but still fall short. Daniel's stand had political ramifications but it was first based on glorifying God.

As Christians, this must be our highest priority. Our stand will have political ramifications but it must be a biblical stand as we commit our allegiance to God above all others.

What does that look like? We must continue to grow in His Word. Being aware of what is happening in the world is not a substitute for growing in God's Word. Biblical illiteracy plagues our churches and starves our discipleship.

The last chapters of this book will help us center our lives around God's truth. He tells us how to be prepared for what we are facing today. We must discover what He says so that we can live confidently in this chaotic world.

Before we arrive at those solutions, we will expose dangers rising today. We must continue to open our eyes and ears to the mindset creeping into our culture. Just like with Daniel's battle, this war is not fought with physical weapons. Currently, it is fought with words. Let's see how words are used to shift our thinking and to usher in the one-world system.

WORLD WAR ON WORDS

What do the words "terrible" and "meat" have in common? Don't worry. This is not an anti-steak rant. These are two English words that have changed meaning over time.

In the King James Version of the Bible, it tells us Nehemiah prayed to God, "And said, I beseech thee, O LORD God of heaven, the great and terrible God, that keepeth covenant and mercy for them that love him and observe his commandments" (Neh. 1:5).

What comes to mind when you see the word "terrible" in this verse? Our modern concept of this word has only negative connotations. However, when the KJV was first translated in 1611, "terrible" meant "standing in awe." Today, we would say something like, "The great and awesome God."

"Meat" has gone through similar changes. We read in the Creation account, "And God said, Behold, I have given you every herb bearing seed, which is upon the face of all the earth, and every tree, in the which is the fruit of a tree yielding seed; to you it shall be for meat" (Gen. 1:29).

We think of "meat" as beef, pork, poultry, and fish. Clearly, it does not mean that in this verse. Back in 1611, "meat" meant solid food, so we could understand this verse to say, "It shall be for food."

Language is constantly changing. However, certain terms are being manipulated intentionally. A war is being waged with words. This is no small issue of semantics. I want to show you a purposeful usage of keywords and terms that reveal how this war is being fought.

A Christian commercial aired during the 2023 NFL Super Bowl as part of an ad campaign called, "He Gets Us." The campaign attempted to demonstrate the humanity of Jesus. U.S. Rep. Alexandria Ocasio-Cortez, popularly known as AOC, posted her thoughts about the ad on her Twitter account, "Something tells me Jesus would *not* spend millions of dollars on Super Bowl ads to make fascism look benign."

Set aside the debates over Jesus for a second and focus on her use of the term "fascism." Historically, fascism describes a domineering dictatorship fueled by intense nationalism and often involving racism.

Rep. Ocasio-Cortez reveals the approach of globalists. Anyone who does not go along with the globalist agenda will be labeled a fascist. They are intentionally changing the definition of this term to oppose any voices who do not agree with their agenda.

Anyone, like the makers of this Super Bowl commercial, who even suggests that Jesus is the answer to the division in our country is labeled a fascist. Anyone who thinks the American government should put the needs of our nation ahead of other nations is labeled a fascist.

This is not just my conjecture, nor was this a one-time occurrence. AOC has continued to throw out the term fascist. About a month after the 2023 Super Bowl, she cried fascism when the GOP presented a Parents Bill of Rights in the U.S. House of Representatives. This legislation sought to ensure parents knew what their kids were being taught in public schools and that their voices would be heard if they opposed what was being taught.

While opposing the Parents Bill of Rights, she accused the Republicans of bringing culture wars into the classrooms. However, cultural values are always being taught in the classroom. The real question is, "Whose cultural values are being taught?"

She is fighting in this culture war to ensure her values are taught in the classroom and any opposing voices are silenced. In her remarks against the Parents Bill of Rights, she said that she values "freedom over fascism." We must ask a crucial question, "Whose freedom does she value?" Only those whose values align with hers. Now, we must ask another important question, "Who is acting more like a fascist?"

She is not alone in using fascism in this manner. Students for Life has many student-led, pro-life chapters on college and university campuses across America. The chapter at Virginia Commonwealth University in Richmond, Virginia hosted an on-campus meeting with some nationally known speakers in March 2023. Pro-abortion supporters showed up to protest and chanted, "Fascists go home." Campus security shut the event down because of the violent outburst.

Central to the pro-abortion protesters' message was the term, fascists. They employ this word with the same emphasis as Rep. Ocasio-Cortez. This is a tactic the liberal left uses to brand anyone who does not go along with their agenda and values.

They want to vilify anyone who disagrees with them. They use words like fascists to bring guilt and shame upon their opposition. One of the great powers of words is repetition. The more terms like fascist that are used in this manner, the more people will come to understand fascism in a new way. Thus, the definition of this term is intentionally changed and weaponized in the culture wars.

Fascism is not the only term we must recognize. This war on words is fought with specific terms. The sooner we open our eyes to how these terms are used, the better we will be able to recognize what is happening under our noses.

"Cooperation"

The term "cooperation" is a great illustration of this point. The World Economic Forum is a community comprised of elite influencers and leaders from across the globe. I will share more about them in a later chapter. The theme for their 2023 forum was "Cooperation in a Fragmented World."[4]

How they used the term "cooperation" throughout their statement reveals they define it as the opposite of competition. In their thinking, the only way for our world to survive and advance is to come together as one. They argue businesses can no longer afford to think only of their business or their industry. They must see themselves as part of the global whole. For example, an automotive manufacturer must not only consider its business, but it must also see itself as part of the solution for global workforce issues, healthcare issues, and climate change issues.

In this mindset, businesses must learn to cooperate with each sector. The WEF urged people to stop thinking about individual sectors and begin thinking about the global whole. They yearn to bring divergent sectors together. They believe the only way to solve our complex problems is with globally uniting solutions. This unification describes their usage of cooperation.

I am not trying to be anti-cooperation. I think cooperation can be a tremendous blessing. In my ministry, I have sought out authentic biblical cooperation.

---

4   World Economic Forum. (2023, January 16-20). "World Economic Forum Annual Meeting." https://www.weforum.org/events/world-economic-forum-annual-meeting-2023/about/meeting-overview

However, how they use the term cooperation is shifting the definition of this term. Let me give you an example to explain.

What happened about a month after the 2023 WEF Annual Meeting further demonstrates how it is strategically used to promote a global agenda. President Joe Biden announced his intentions to sign a treaty for the U.S. to cooperate with the United Nation's World Health Organization in future pandemic decision-making.

Some media outlets reported that Biden had surrendered U.S. sovereignty as he pledged away America's ability to make its own decisions in a pandemic. However, USA Today quickly labeled this characterization as "false information."[5]

So, on the one hand, USA Today said this was not true, but on the other hand, they used the word cooperation to slide it under our noses. You see, President Biden was referring to an accord drafted by the U.S. regarding the response to future pandemics.

USA Today interviewed one of the authors of this accord, Lawrence Gostin. USA Today quoted Gostin in response to their so-called "false information." He said, "The treaty would seek global cooperation in preventing and responding to a pandemic." He was quick to add the WHO wouldn't gain any power over states if this accord is accepted.

This doublespeak is contagious. One month, the World Economic Forum is touting "Cooperation in a Fragmented World." The next month, the U.S. president is touting cooperation in a global pandemic. A "nothing to see here" attitude pervades these events.

When people tried to share articles about President Biden's apparent surrender of U.S. sovereignty, Facebook and Instagram labeled them "False Information" and blocked others from seeing them. Guess who paid the fact-checkers at USA Today to label information as false? The wonderful folks at Facebook and Instagram! At the bottom of the USA Today article it reads, "Our fact-check work is supported in part by a grant from Facebook."[6] You cannot make this stuff up!

---

5   Kochi, Sudiksha. (2023, February 23) "Fact check: False claim that pandemic accord gives WHO control over US pandemic policies." USA TODAY. https://www.usatoday.com/story/news/factcheck/2023/02/23/fact-check-false-claim-us-sovereignty-and-who-accord/11313805002/

6   Ibid.

Rise of the One-World Mind

"Cooperation" is such a nice-sounding word. It typically does not set off alarms in our minds, and that is one of the reasons it is a weapon of choice in the global war of words. Its subtlety is its stealthy strength. They want us to think the U.S. is not giving up sovereignty, it is simply "cooperating globally" in future pandemics.

"Global" and "Local"

The terms "global" and "local" seem straightforward and harmless. However, these terms become deadly when mixed with brainwashing techniques.

Thinking globally is to put the needs of the planet first. By that, I do not mean putting only the needs of other people first. Gore demonstrated this well as he proclaimed his global climate-change warning.

Thinking locally is anything less than thinking globally. For example, putting the needs of your nation ahead of the globe is thinking locally. Putting the needs of your family ahead of someone halfway around the world is thinking locally. Putting the needs of your community ahead of another's is thinking locally.

The global elites use guilt and shame to shift the public perception. In their view, thinking locally is small-minded and selfish. They use rhetoric like, "The fate of the world is in our hands." They urge us to stop being selfish and small-minded and get with the global program.

I do not want to come across as cantankerous without a cause. Christians should be model citizens. Christians should show love to others and be good stewards of this planet. Selfishness is sinful.

However, using guilt and shame to manipulate the masses is unbiblical and ungodly. Global thinking is marketed as the only path to humanity's survival. This is just a cloak for their real goal—control.

This is one of the most important truths I hope you take away from this book. The globalists are not thinking with your best interests at heart. They want control. They mix the term "global" into their brainwashing propaganda to convince you it is best for you.

Returning to my example of a global monetary system, we will be sold messages like, "Buy and sell anything from anyone at any time with your global digital currency." Or, "Global investing is seamlessly available to everyone with the new global currency." However, a singular global digital currency will give one group total control over the total finances of every person on Earth. If there is no cash, they will be able to see every transaction, and they could control every way you use money. Buyer beware!

"Stakeholder"

"Stakeholder" is another subtle term to watch for. In the past, businesses spoke of their responsibility to shareholders. Now stakeholder is the term of choice. These terms appear synonymous, but don't let appearances fool you.

"Stakeholder" is a much broader term than "shareholder." A shareholder owns shares in a company. The shareholder makes money when the business does well and loses money when the business does poorly. Thus, a shareholder wants the individual business to thrive.

A stakeholder could be a third-party vendor who works with a company. This stakeholder would want to see the business succeed because that often means more business for this third-party vendor.

However, the government could also be considered a stakeholder. They have a stake in the business because that business produces one of the government's favorite words – taxes. The business pays corporate taxes and each employee of that company pays payroll taxes. Both the company and each employee in turn pay sales taxes when they make purchases in the marketplace.

The World Economic Forum heavily uses "stakeholder" in describing its global goals. For example, the war in Ukraine began in 2022. The WEF offered their global solution, "The geopolitical vane turned from cooperation to competition. There is a growing need for a new global system that is more stakeholder based and equipped to handle the dynamics of the 21st century."[7]

This statement uses both "stakeholder" and "cooperation" in the same sentence. Let's consider how they use cooperation in this sentence, then return to their use of stakeholder.

In the eyes of the WEF, war is competition. But their view of competition between countries goes far beyond war. If a nation puts the needs of its citizens ahead of another nation's, then they are competitive instead of cooperative.

---

7   World Economic Forum. (2023, January 16-20) "World Economic Forum Annual Meeting." https://www.weforum.org/events/world-economic-forum-annual-meeting-2023/about/meeting-overview

The border security debate reveals two competing (if I can use that anti-globalist word) ideologies. The globalists want a borderless world, while those who put their country first want some level of border security and a better process of legal immigration.

Some may see this as a battle between globalists and nationalists. In some cases, it is. However, patriotism is not the same as nationalism. One can patriotically desire the betterment of their country while still being good neighbors with other nations.

Neighbors can get along well with each other and visit as often as they like, but at the end of the day, both neighbors have their own place to live. Globalists want to tear down the walls of separation and bring everyone together in one massive global house. The WEF's use of the term "cooperation" signals the movement in this direction. They view us all as "stakeholders" in this new global system they wish to create.

If we do not go along with their agenda, then we are not a good neighbor. Therefore, we are not global stakeholders who seek the overall good of the world. The shame game will be used against those who think locally before thinking globally.

Lest you think I am only talking about my theories of what may happen, I will let you in on an open secret, it is already happening.

Did you know that many American colleges and universities are openly promoting global citizenship? It is in their mission statements and programs. Some schools even have centers for global citizenship. Students are told they are stakeholders in the new global frontier.

Global citizenship is championed while American citizenship is vilified. Students are taught, "Your national citizenship is an accident. Your global citizenship is a choice." American youth and college students are fed a steady diet of this philosophy as they are encouraged to become global citizens.

American history and civics are not being taught at a proficient level in American high schools and higher education. The Woodrow Wilson Foundation found that "only four in 10 Americans can pass a 20-question test based on questions from the U.S. citizenship exam. Even more disturbing, only 27 percent of those under the age of 45 nationally can demonstrate a basic understanding of American history."[8]

Our education system is intentionally ignoring American history and civics to usher in a new generation of global stakeholders. We have to open our eyes to what is happening all around us.

"Climate Change"

Isn't it interesting how we transitioned from "global warming" to "climate change?" The strength of the term climate change is its vagueness. This term can be weaponized to scare people into submission.

It is the scapegoat for many of the world's problems. As I noted earlier, Al Gore blamed climate change for the immigration crises many nations are facing. However, climate change does not necessarily equal poverty.

It is outside the scope of this section to provide a treatise on the scientific perspectives of climate change. That is a whole other book to be written. However, I must mention something about climate change science to show you it is not as settled as some claim.

The fact is, the climate is constantly changing. This is not new. It is as old as the Earth itself. There have been warming and cooling periods in Earth's history. Scientists tell us, "Historical records indicate there were several warm periods including the medieval warm period (MWP) between A.D. 900 and 1300 in which people were able to farm in Greenland—an area currently covered in ice."[9]

Any meteorologist worth their mettle will tell you we have just scratched the surface in weather studies. There is much we do not know about the climate and severe weather systems.

It is irresponsible to panic people about climate change when you cannot figure out whether we are in a period of global warming. But this is not about the climate. It is about control. There is a storm brewing, but it is a combination of factors to create the opportunity to grab control.

Open your eyes and ears to these key terms that are filling media today. New

8   Patrick Riccards. (2019, May 7) "Report: Why Americans Don't Know Their History and How to Change It." Woodrow Wilson Foundation. https://woodrow.org/news/american-history-report/

9   Jessica Jaworski and Avery Foley. (2023, January 24) "Climate Alarmism: Five Scientific Reasons Not to Panic About Climate Change." Answers in Genesis. https://answersingenesis.org/environmental-science/climate-alarmism/

terms will come around, so be alert. See through the deception and warn others about the coming storm. But do not fight fear with fear and panic with panic. Do not be a casualty of the world war on words. Remember, our response must be biblical.

God reveals that during the Great Tribulation, there will be a one-world system of government, economy, and worship. How do we see the mindset behind each of these rising in our world today? The next three chapters will explore these areas in depth.

RISE OF THE ONE-WORLD GOVERNMENT MINDSET

The one-world government mindset is rising before our eyes. We need to open our eyes to what is happening around us. There are too many blind sheep who are following the one-world agenda without asking any questions. Clever marketing sells us shiny new stuff with all its glittering promises. If we are not careful, we could ignore the serious downside to our peril.

Consider this true story as an illustration of that fact. A man had a smart home equipped with all the latest automated gadgets, powered by Amazon. An Amazon delivery driver approached the door with his headphones in. The digital doorbell offered a standard automated greeting. The driver mistakenly thought he heard a racist comment, so he reported the alleged act of racism to Amazon. The homeowner was not even home at the time, but Amazon decided to lock down his account and his smart devices based on the driver's report. This man was locked out of his own home for one week while he argued his innocence with Amazon. Once he offered sufficient proof, they unlocked his account and his home.

The promises of the shiny, new stuff seemed to open new horizons for this homeowner until it backfired horribly. Clever government marketing sells our world shiny new promises. We need to pause and consider the serious implications of going down this pathway before we agree to something we may live to regret. If I were this homeowner, I would be removing these "smart" devices as soon as possible.

What are some of these shiny new opportunities? How do they tie together? What are the concerns we need to be aware of? How could it promote a one-world government system?

Thousands of years ago, the Bible predicted what is rising in our world today. During the Great Tribulation, an unholy trinity will rule over Earth. Satan, the Antichrist, and the False Prophet will form this evil alliance. Revelation 13:7b describes the scope of the Antichrist's political power: "and power was given him over all kindreds, and tongues, and nations." This end-times power bloc will dominate government, worship, and the economy. Over the next few chapters, we will explore how we see this mindset rising right now.

I need to give an important disclaimer before we move forward. I am not saying technology is evil. It is a tool. Any tool can be used for good or evil. A hammer can be used to build a house or hit someone over the head. Thus, the tool is dependent upon the one controlling it. Our ministry utilizes all sorts of technology to share God's Good News. Just because I mention a certain type of technology in this book does not mean we should avoid it altogether.

For example, using current technological payment systems is not the same as receiving the mark of the beast (Rev. 13:16-18). The church will not be on Earth when the Antichrist comes to power or when the mark of the beast is deployed, so we do not have to worry about using or receiving the mark of the beast.

So, if Christians will not be on Earth for the Great Tribulation, why should we be concerned about these things? Why should we be aware of these concepts?

Consider three reasons why we ought to be aware and concerned. First, many around us are not ready for the rapture. Knowing these truths ought to fire up our evangelistic zeal to share Jesus while we have a window of opportunity.

Secondly, Christians ought to live with our focus on eternity. The world lives for the here and the now, but Christians are called to walk with eternity in mind.

Thirdly, understanding these truths helps the church keep our focus on what is both eternally and urgently important. We have a God-given window of opportunity to impact this world for eternity. Otherwise, we would already be with Him in heaven. We have a responsibility to speak the truth in love and shine Christ's light in the darkness.

I do not want my brothers and sisters in Christ to respond with panic and fear to the rising one-world system. There is a difference between fearful worrying and righteous concern. However, we must open our eyes to what is happening. We must pray for God to open the eyes of others so they can see His light in this dark world.

For a few years of my ministry, I ignored this kind of stuff as "crazy, conspiracy talk" until my eyes were opened through my study. I then felt like the proverbial ostrich with its head in the sand. I was in my little bubble, ignoring how God's truth was coming alive in the world around me. I was unaware of how God was advancing His plan for the ages during my lifetime.

As I expose the mindset pervading our world today, I pray your eyes will be open so that you will see God's truth come alive, too. Armed with this understanding, explore with me how God's plan is unfolding through the rise of the one-world government mindset.

The Rise of Digital Government

Governments are quickly going digital. This move is accompanied by a long list of promises for citizens. Who likes to wait in line at a government agency that is only open for about eight hours a day Monday through Friday? What if you could complete almost every government transaction from anywhere at any time convenient for you? American citizens would no longer need to worry about differences from state to state. It would all be standardized and user-friendly.

Oh, and by the way, these new options will reduce fraud and offer greater security to you. Further, you will help the government save money which could lower taxes. As a bonus, you will help the environment since the government is less reliant on paper and plastic with the switch to digital. Did someone say, "Climate change?"

So far, it sounds like a win-win. Ooh, shiny new stuff! Before we look at some potential problems with this digital push, consider how we see this happening in our world today.

Going Global with Digital Identification

Digital identification is quickly gaining ground across the world. Before the ink is dry on this page, nations will have advanced their technological pursuits. That is why I hesitate to share too much information about what a single country is doing. But you need to know the kinds of things that are happening around the world so that you will be awake when plans are announced.

Denmark is one of the world leaders in the digital government push. They have developed a government ID program, called "MitID," which is Danish for "My ID." Having this digital ID unlocks citizens' access to education, insurance, utilities, banking, healthcare, and taxes.[10]

On the other side of the world, South Korea, also called the Republic of Korea, is constantly advancing its digital government. By 2025, they hope to use

---

10 Danish Agency for Digital Government. (2023, June 19) https://en.digst.dk/systems/mitid/

chat-bots and Artificial Intelligence assistants to communicate with citizens. They also want to have a mobile digital ID that authenticates citizens' IDs using technology like biometrics. As they push toward these goals, they also want to achieve international cooperation as they support digital governments in developing countries.[11]

Australia also has a mobile app called MyGovID.[12] This mobile app uses the smartphone's built-in facial recognition or fingerprint scans to verify the user as an additional security measure.

This app features three different tiers of access to services based on the principle, that the more you give the more you get. To move from "basic" to "standard," Australians must verify their identity by uploading a government ID or passport. Then, to move up to the highest tier, the app uses facial recognition to scan the user's face, and then crosschecks the face scan to the uploaded ID photo. This one-time process is all that is needed to gain access to Australia's digital government offerings.

Imagine a world where you can almost eliminate trips to government buildings and a seemingly never-ending carousel of running from office to office. That in itself is enough to elicit the "Ooh, shiny new stuff!" response. However, what happens when this tool falls into the wrong hands? What if it was used to track or control people?

What happens when someone voices displeasure with the ruling powers? Just like the man locked out of his home by Amazon when he was reported as a racist, would someone reported to the government be locked out of access to utilities, education, or healthcare? We must consider these things before signing up for the shiny new stuff.

For my fellow Americans reading these facts, we may be tempted to think, "Oh, that's happening in other countries. We do not have to worry about it." But is that true? It may shock you to know America is one of the world leaders in the push toward digital government. In United Nations' 2022 rankings, the U.S. was number ten in the world. Australia ranked seventh. South Korea

---

11 South Korea Ministry of the Interior and Safety. (Accessed June 19, 2023) "Digital Government Masterplan 2021-2025." Ministry of the Interior and Safety. https://www.dgovkorea.go.kr/ under "Digital Government Masterplan 2021-25"

12 Australian Government. (Accessed June 19, 2023) "myGovID." https://www.mygovid.gov.au/

ranked third. Denmark ranked first.[13] America is moving in the same direction as these other countries.

That is a big claim to make, so let me back it up with some evidence. I was speaking about some of this information and a certified public accountant approached me afterward. She told me I needed to know what the IRS required some of her clients to do. The IRS required them to register with the ID.me website and upload their government-issued photo ID to validate their identity.

As I began to check out the IRS website ID.me, I discovered the IRS had walked back from its initial policy and made biometric registration voluntary instead of mandatory to complete certain transactions. But in the same document, the IRS stated it is joining the efforts of other government agencies to build authentication tools into the new platform, Login.gov, and move away from its ID.me.[14]

I encourage you to visit the website Login.gov and check out its expanding features for yourself. It is touted as the American public's one account for government. Guess what? Some agencies require ID confirmation before giving you access to their digital services. So, on the one hand, the IRS seems to be backing off its stringent ID requirements, but on the other, they are finding different channels to accomplish the same goal.

Is America moving toward a digital ID system like the other nations in the U.N.'s Top 10? Many individual American states have either launched or are developing digital ID options. When several states start doing something, the federal government gets involved too. Legislation is in process in both the U.S. House of Representatives and Senate to give a standardized format for states to improve digital identity. The bills have received bipartisan support but have not yet passed into law as of this writing.[15]

---

13 United Nations. (Accessed June 19, 2023) "2022 E-Government Development Index." https://publicadministration.un.org/egovkb/en-us/data-center

14 I.R.S. (2022, February 21) "IRS Statement – New features put in place for IRS Online Account Registration; process strengthened to ensure privacy and security." I.R.S. https://www.irs.gov/newsroom/irs-statement-new-features-put-in-place-for-irs-online-account-registration-process-strengthened-to-ensure-privacy-and-security

15 In the U.S. House of Representatives, Bill H.R. 4258 "Improving Digital Identity Act of 2021" did not pass the House, but it is typically reintroduced yearly by Democratic Rep. Bill Foster of Illinois and his colleagues. In the U.S. Senate, Bill S. 884 "Improving Digital Identity Act of 2023" was introduced by Independent Senator Kyrsten Sinema from Arizona and co-sponsored by Republican Senator Cynthia Lummis from Wyoming. These bills can be read by searching for them on the website Congress.gov.

My goal for this section is not to give you news but to help you understand how our world governments are pushing toward similar goals by similar means. Digital IDs offer many promises and advantages including reducing fraud and identity theft. But you may be wondering, "How do digital IDs move us closer to a one-world government system?"

Consider another promise – digital IDs will help solve border security crises across the world.

Border Security and Digital ID

How can digital IDs help solve the border security crises our world is facing? Imagine everyone in the world has a digital ID linked with their biometric data, such as facial recognition software or a fingerprint scan. It would be much easier for nations to track who is entering their country.

If the police arrest someone who is not carrying any identification, they could simply take a picture of the suspect and identify him in a centralized database. A body camera could serve the same purpose. But go a step further. Police and intelligence agencies could use facial recognition cameras and technology mounted throughout our streets to search for criminals.

Some of you may be rolling your eyes thinking, "There he goes again with more wild speculation." That is where you are wrong.

France already allows police investigators and intelligence services to use remote biometric identification to track down terrorists, missing children, and other serious criminals.[16] Facial recognition cameras and technology are already on the market. You can buy a personal security camera system for your home that utilizes facial recognition software.

While I see some wonderful advantages of using this technology, like protecting our families, stopping terrorist attacks, and finding missing children, we must consider its usage from all angles.

Mark it down: As each nation inches closer to digital IDs, we will increasingly hear the need for a single worldwide database of all people. We will continue to hear many of the promises I discussed – safety, security, and greater freedom for all people.

---

16 Borak, Masha. (2023, June 14) "French Senate votes in favor of public facial recognition pilot." Biometric Update. https://www.biometricupdate.com/202306/french-senate-votes-in-favor-of-public-facial-recognition-pilot

Globalist government leaders will continue to allow immigrants to illegally enter their countries so that they can offer their best solution – a borderless world with a digital ID for all people. Biometric data, such as facial recognition, could easily allow people to move about a world with open borders.

"More wild speculation," you may be thinking. Friends, it is happening now. I will discuss this more in the next chapter, but biometric data is rapidly becoming the way we pay, enter, and identify ourselves.

"Take me out to the ballgame," we cheer. Did you know facial recognition ticketing is in high demand for venues and stadiums across America? Your face can be your ticket to enter stadiums and venues across America.

While we may begin to think of the "Ooh, shiny new stuff" promises, there are drawbacks to using this technology. As a powerful tool, whoever controls the tool controls who enters and who buys and sells. Let me give you another true story as an example.

Facial recognition aided an act of revenge against some 90 law firms pursuing litigation against the company that operates Madison Square Garden, home of the New York Knicks and Rangers teams. James Dolan is the CEO of Madison Square Garden and owns both professional sports teams. He banned certain lawyers who work for these firms from attending games by using facial recognition technology. These sports fans bought tickets but were denied entry based on a personal vendetta by Dolan and his staff.[17]

Now, let's return to our future worldwide ID controlled by a globalist government. What happens when someone is flagged by a biometric system based on the decision of the global elites? Access to places and finances could easily be cut off. Remember, Amazon locked a man out of his own home based on their control over their technology.

While technology promises some powerful upgrades and could open new horizons, we cannot fail to ask some crucial questions. Who owns the rights to our scans? Does our face become government property? What happens when the control of this technology falls into the wrong hands, like the Antichrist?

While I wish I could end the chapter here and tell you this is the only way we are

---

17 Office of the New York State Attorney General Letitia James. (2023, January 25) "Attorney General James Seeks Information from Madison Square Garden Regarding Use of Facial Recognition Technology to Deny Entry to Venues." New York State Attorney General. https://ag.ny.gov/press-release/2023/attorney-general-james-seeks-information-madison-square-garden-regarding-use

moving toward a one-world government, I cannot because it is not. Consider the push toward global healthcare solutions.

Going Global with Healthcare

When there is a one-world government, it stands to reason that government-sponsored healthcare will also be global. We are already moving in that direction.

The WHO continues to expand its powerful reach as the global health arm of the U.N. In Chapter 2, I shared how President Biden pledged U.S. cooperation with the WHO in any future pandemics to promote a global response to pandemics.

In a further push toward global healthcare, the WHO maintains a listing of disease classifications. The term for this manual is the International Classification of Diseases. When the 11th revision came out in 2022, it marked the first time the database was fully electronic.[18] As of this writing, the U.S. is still using the ICD-10 coding but is moving toward adapting the 11th revision.

What does this mean for you and me? Soon all of our medical records could be digitized and available worldwide to healthcare providers. If I am traveling in Africa, it could be helpful for medical personnel to have quick access to all my health information in the event of an emergency. But once again I find myself asking what happens when this information falls into the wrong hands or is used in improper manners.

What if I refuse to accept some future vaccine or medical treatment that is made mandatory? My freedoms could be severely limited. I'm sure this does not sound too far-fetched to those who opposed the COVID vaccine mandates.

The WHO has proposed amendments to its International Health Regulations to give them much more control over future pandemics.[19] If these proposals pass, the WHO would gain the authority to force U.N. member states to follow its recommendations in a future health emergency.

For example, you could face very real consequences for not receiving any vaccine or treatment the WHO authorizes. What kind of consequences? Global Health Passports, if authorized, could restrict your ability to travel if you do

18 World Health Organization. (Accessed 2023, June 25). "ICD-11 Fact Sheet." https://icd.who.int/en/docs/icd11factsheet_en.pdf

19 Bell, David (2023, February 16). "The proposed amendments to WHO's International Health Regulations, their implications for individual and national sovereignty." Pandata. https://pandata.org/proposed-amendments-whos-ihr/

not have the proper vaccinations. Further, the WHO could authorize states to identify and isolate individuals who refuse to comply. I cannot believe I am writing this – the WHO's proposals would grant them authority to force people to get medical examinations, medications, and vaccinations.

The WHO also proposes that all member-states stop the spread of false information via media, social networks, and other means. It seems like the uproar President Biden created with his WHO cooperation pledge contained more truth than conspiracy. Books like this could be banned if the WHO has its way. Websites and channels dedicated to exposing their agenda could be shut down.

The WHO director-general would have the power to single-handedly declare a global health emergency based solely on a potential outbreak under the new proposals. The director-general would not have to gain the approval of any other person, nation, or board to enact a global health emergency declaration.

Whether these proposals pass, the mere promotion of them demonstrates the direction the WHO wants to take global healthcare. It seeks control over every person on Earth. I hope you see how easily this kind of power could be turned against the world in the biblical end-times scenario. The one-world healthcare system is rising before our eyes.

Did you know the WHO has an initiative called One Health? It seeks to optimize the health of people, animals, and the environment. As you read this section, you may be prone to think about how the WHO could create a global healthcare crisis like the COVID-19 pandemic. However, it could just as easily declare a global health crisis based on climate change (there is that term again).

If the global health branch of the United Nations is moving in this direction, you can be sure the U.N. is as well.

Going Global with the United Nations

The U.N. was founded in 1945 to help foster peace and cooperation among nations. The U.N. is united with organizations like the World Economic Forum. These groups are working together to realize their vision for our future. In 2015, the U.N. announced its pursuit of Agenda 2030. This agenda includes seventeen sustainable development goals for every nation they hope to reach by 2030.[20]

20 United Nations Department of Economic and Social Affairs. (Accessed 2023, July 25). "Transforming our world: the 2030 Agenda for Sustainable Development." United Nations. https://sdgs.un.org/2030agenda

These seventeen targets include items like no poverty, zero hunger, good health and well-being, quality education, and access to clean water and sanitation. Only a heartless person would say these are bad goals. I do not want anyone going hungry anywhere in the world. I dare say the Christian worldview has done more to advance aid to the poor than any other worldview. Helping the hungry is noble.

However, massive questions are hanging in the air. First, how do we define the terms? Let's look at just one of the seventeen targets as an example – zero hunger. How will we know when there is zero hunger on Earth? Is there a way to measure this goal?

The U.N. spells out the answer for us in their Agenda 2030. For the goal to "end hunger, achieve food security and improved nutrition and promote sustainable agriculture," they list five goals with three action steps.

The first two goals to end hunger are what you might expect. They want to eliminate malnutrition by giving people year-round access to nutritious food.

Their third goal to end hunger is subtle, so I want to unpack it for you. Here is what it says,

"By 2030, double the agricultural productivity and incomes of small-scale food producers, in particular women, indigenous peoples, family farmers, pastoralists and fishers, including through secure and equal access to land, other productive resources and inputs, knowledge, financial services, markets and opportunities for value addition and non-farm employment."[21]

Notice they want to double the income for the people groups listed by giving them "secure and equal access to land…[and] financial services." Friends, this is blatant Marxist communism! The way they want to end hunger is by redistributing the wealth and by taking away private property ownership. They do not hide their plan. It is there for all to see.

Is it not curious that the last line of this goal says they want to double the agricultural productivity and incomes through "non-farm employment"? How do you improve food production by moving people out of farm employment?

That is a big question that leads to a couple of other major topics – climate change and artificial intelligence. Simply stated, AI and other technological advances could push humans out of the agricultural job market almost entirely.

---

21 Ibid.

The climate change agenda also plays a major role in the global government. The fourth goal to end hunger states:

"By 2030, ensure sustainable food production systems and implement resilient agricultural practices that increase productivity and production, that help maintain ecosystems, that strengthen capacity for adaptation to climate change, extreme weather, drought, flooding and other disasters and that progressively improve land and soil quality[.]"[22]

European farmers face an existential crisis due to increasing climate change restrictions. Multi-generational family farmers wonder if they will be forced to close due to climate restrictions placed on them.

Climate change permeates the entire 2030 Agenda. As I wrote previously, "climate change" is such an ambiguous term it could be wielded to promote or defend anything. Al Gore and the WEF are using it to create guilt and fear so that people will get on board with their globalist government agenda.

My wife and daughter like to bake on occasion. I was surprised to learn that salt is often an ingredient in many cakes. Just about every recipe in a cookbook sprinkles salt in somewhere. So, too, climate change is sprinkled into every globalist agenda. Anytime the global government elites need to motivate people to action, they sprinkle in "climate change." But this is a communistic recipe for disaster.

The U.N. is actively working toward a global government with communist values. They are working hand in hand with groups like the WEF to promote this agenda across the world.

In the biblical end-times scenario, the Antichrist will rule over the one-world government and can control people's lives (Rev. 13). God's Word is clear. When the short-lived global empire rises, it will dominate the lives of everyone alive during the Great Tribulation.

The Antichrist could easily rise to power out of this kind of global-government system. Will our world meet these goals by 2030? Time will tell.

Before we get distracted by the shiny, new stuff promised by a global government, we must open our eyes to what hides behind the promises. Digital IDs and border crises could usher in global citizenship and eventually eliminate national borders.

22 Ibid.

Healthcare is quickly becoming interconnected digitally and internationally. The WHO is actively seeking greater control and power over international health decision-making.

Groups like the U.N. and WEF are establishing agendas to move our world into a global whole. The economy is increasingly international and tests are underway to move to a central bank digital currency. Examine this vital information with me in the next chapter.

RISE OF THE ONE-WORLD ECONOMIC MINDSET

A global digital currency looms on the horizon. Technology is quickly changing the economy and global elites are advancing their economic vision. I know how far-fetched that sounds, so let me show you how each of these statements is true.

Bible prophecy describes a one-world economy during the Great Tribulation. Revelation 13:16-18 describes this system under the Antichrist's rule:

> And he causeth all, both small and great, rich and poor, free and bond, to receive a mark in their right hand, or in their foreheads: And that no man might buy or sell, save he that had the mark, or the name of the beast, or the number of his name. Here is wisdom. Let him that hath understanding count the number of the beast: for it is the number of a man; and his number is Six hundred threescore and six.

In this popular passage, we are told everyone on Earth will have to receive this mark of the beast to buy or sell anything. His number is the infamous 666.

Whenever I heard about the mark of the beast as a child, I tended to think about people having trouble shopping for groceries. Those who resist the mark of the beast will never see the inside of a restaurant or grocery store again unless someone else is paying. However, that is merely the beginning of their problems. Without the mark of the beast, people will have no access to housing, medicine, healthcare, transportation, or food. Imagine life without access to utilities like water and electricity.

Think for just a minute how many modern conveniences require electricity. As I write this, the air conditioning in our building is messing up, so it is turned off. It is the middle of summer and the temperature inside the building is nearly 90 degrees. Most of my ministry colleagues have taken their work to another part of the building where the air conditioning is working. Only a couple of us are sweating it out. It becomes increasingly harder to not join them. I find myself asking, "Why am I putting myself through this?" Those who try to avoid the mark of the beast will face even greater pressure to conform and will constantly wonder why they are resisting.

Think about how many of our communications depend upon utilities. Internet, mobile phones, computers, and telephones will be unavailable to those who do not get the mark of the beast.

Anyone who does not receive this mark will be forced to live completely off the grid in a very primitive manner. They will have no access to money since all currency will be centralized and digital. They will be completely cut off from the economy unless they can find someone willing to barter goods and services in exchange for food, medicine, or access to utilities.

With the rise of facial recognition tools as discussed in Chapter 3, would these non-compliant people be able to show their face in public at all? I doubt it. I shudder to think about the possibility of special camps or prisons being set up to quarantine the non-compliant people.

During the Great Tribulation, people will not have an option. The Bible makes it clear that everyone will be forced to have the mark of the beast. Those who resist will be breaking the law. The Antichrist's one-world economy will make it virtually impossible to survive without his mark of the beast.

How can the Antichrist control the economy worldwide? The move to a digital currency may initially give us the "ooh, shiny new stuff" vibe with all its promised convenience. However, since the name of the game is control, a centralized digital currency gives the powerful elites all the control they need to get humanity in line with their agenda.

If the currency is digital and cashless, there will be no more anonymity in transactions. Anything and everything you use your money for will be recorded. Plus, it will be much easier to control how people use money by denying transactions between certain parties.

"Oh, that will never happen!" you might object. Some banks have canceled the accounts of Christian organizations over their moral standards. For example, J.P. Morgan canceled the bank accounts of the Family Research Council. This ignited a legal battle, but my point is to show what can happen at the whim of the controlling economic power if they decide to restrict or cancel your access to funds.

If all money is digital and under the watch of a central bank, could they not simply cancel the accounts for individuals or groups whom they do not like? Could they not control access to and usage of those funds?

What happens when a "climate change emergency" compels those in power to decide we can no longer purchase gasoline with our digital currency? Our gas-powered equipment will instantly become scrap metal. What if a global lockdown hits, such as we experienced in 2020, and the authorities decide we must remain within a five-block radius of our home? They could digitally set a limit on any purchases we make to keep us from buying anything beyond our five-block radius or from entering any place beyond that radius.

These are possibilities that I do not like to consider but we must think about potential consequences before buying into the shiny new stuff. A totally digital monetary system provides enormous opportunities for banks to control how funds are used.

Are countries moving toward a central bank digital currency (CBDC)? The Atlantic Council tracks CBDC development across the globe. Only thirty-five countries were considering a CBDC in May 2020. In three short years, that number skyrocketed to 130 countries, which represented 98 percent of the global gross domestic product (GDP).[23]

As of this writing, the European Central Bank is quickly developing a digital euro. India, Brazil, Australia, China, and Russia are rapidly moving toward a CBDC.

In the U.S., the Federal Reserve researched digital U.S. dollar transactions with some of the nation's largest banks from late 2022 to early 2023. Although more work would need to be done to begin a CBDC in the U.S., the Federal Reserve said the technology is there to enable a digital dollar now.[24] The Federal Reserve's "Project Cedar" is an ongoing multiphase project examining similar digital financial transactions internationally.

To be clear, the Federal Reserve would need congressional approval to transition to a CBDC As of this writing, there is no legislation proposed which would allow a CBDC in the U.S. However, we need to keep our eyes and ears open for any legislation to allow and approve a CBDC.

Why? Because there is an international effort to bring banks together in a united global system. The International Monetary Fund (IMF) launched an international central bank digital currency in 2023 during a meeting in Washington D.C. They envision this currency expediting international transactions between

23 Atlantic Council. (Accessed 2023, November 17) "Central Bank Digital Currency Tracker." https://www.atlanticcouncil.org/cbdctracker/

24 Federal Reserve Bank of New York. (Accessed 2023, July 7) "Facilitating Wholesale Digital Asset Settlement." https://www.newyorkfed.org/aboutthefed/nyic/facilitating-wholesale-digital-asset-settlement

central banks. The IMF announced later in 2023 that it is working on a platform so that central banks can operate as a united global central bank.

The global financial sector continues to move toward both global and digital solutions to simplify complex issues like international currency exchange rates. Technology is shrinking our world, creating a greater demand for a standardized global monetary system.

Did you hear what the country of Ethiopia announced in 2023? By the end of 2024, its national digital ID will be mandatory for all transactions with financial institutions. Our world is inching closer to a one-world economy.[25]

Among the world's top economies, the U.S. is the last holdout from a CBDC There is increasing pressure to bring our nation in line with the rest of the world. Groups like the WEF are promoting their economic vision to fundamentally transform our world.

The World Economic Forum

I have referred to the WEF in just about every chapter up to this point. Entire books are devoted to unmasking the WEF and its founder Klaus Schwab from authors like Pastor Billy Crone. My goal is not to be exhaustive in discussing the WEF, but rather to show how they are aiding the rise of the one-world economy.

For those who may not be aware, the WEF is an annual meeting of some of the world's most powerful and influential leaders. Al Gore, King Charles III, Mark Zuckerberg, and Bill Gates are among some of the WEF notables. Klaus Schwab founded the WEF in 1971 and it has blossomed into a powerful coalition of global elites.

The WEF has a global solution for every issue our planet is facing. They urge the world to stop thinking locally and start thinking globally. Allow me to briefly remind you that, in their minds, thinking locally is anything less than thinking globally. For example, any country that puts the needs of its citizens ahead of another nation's is thinking locally instead of globally. To them, thinking locally is selfish and small-minded.

Would you like to know what the global elites think about you and your local agenda? They think that you do not know what is best for you and your future.

---

25 Macdonald, Ayang. (2023, July 12) "Ethiopia to make digital ID obligatory for banking operations." Biometric Update. https://www.biometricupdate.com/202307/ethiopia-to-make-digital-id-obligatory-for-banking-operations

They think that your house and the stuff you own are selfishly draining the planet of precious resources. They think that gasoline or diesel vehicle you drive, and your unwillingness to switch to an electric vehicle, prove you are both ignorant and selfish.

They think the company you own or work for is selfish if it does not become part of a global solution to stop climate change and end poverty once and for all. Your hunger to consume food from grocery stores and restaurants is putting a burden on our planet that cannot be sustained.

They urge you to open your mind and heart as we move to a global society. The essence of their globalist logic is, "Quit thinking locally and start thinking globally. The top state, science, and business leaders are working hard to foster a global reset to solve our crises. Why can't you just sit down, shut up, and follow what is best for you as a global citizen? Trust the experts. They know what they are doing. Get on board or get left behind."

Ronald Reagan famously said, "The nine most terrifying words in the English language are: I'm from the government, and I'm here to help."[26] When the government gets bigger, our freedoms get smaller.

With my tongue firmly in my cheek, I ask, with the likes of Al Gore and Klaus Schwab cooperating in their globalist agenda with political and business leaders from around the world, why should we be concerned? While they view their role as protectors and advancers of the planet, in reality, they are moving the world toward a one-world system, which is a highlight of the Antichrist's rule during the Great Tribulation period.

The world is being prepared to accept global solutions to our complex global issues. World leaders attending these kinds of forums are being conditioned and pressured to think globally in their decisions.

The Antichrist will eventually take advantage of this conditioned thought pattern as he implements and advances his agenda. With the key economic world leaders on board, the rest of the population will be forced to follow to survive. During the Great Tribulation, it's either get on board or starve.

Would you like to understand how they think and how they want the world to think? Let's look at more of what they said at the 2023 WEF as an example.

---

26 Ronald Reagan Presidential Foundation and Institute. (Accessed 2023, July 12) "August 12, 1986, Reagan Quotes and Speeches." https://www.reaganfoundation.org/ronald-reagan/reagan-quotes-speeches/news-conference-1/

Remember, the theme was "Cooperation in a Fragmented World." The WEF wrote, "The basic tenet of the programme [sic] is the premise that the current crises, as serious as they are, are manifestations of larger systemic deficiencies accrued over time."[27] In other words, the current energy, healthcare, and food crises, for example, happened because of thinking locally instead of globally.

This is further revealed in their very next statement. "They [the current crises] are also the result of a narrow vision of systems as sectors rather than true multidisciplinary, networked entities that are highly dynamic, particularly in the context of the meta trends of the Fourth Industrial Revolution and climate change."

They reason since individuals and businesses tend to look out for their own interests in their small sphere of expertise and influence, we are losing the big picture of how it is all connected. Here comes their peer pressure: the fate of the world depends on whether we will stop being selfish and small-minded, or get with the global program.

Notice what they said: to view whole systems as individual sectors is thinking too narrowly. They do not want world leaders and citizens to think in terms of the parts, such as financial, technology, healthcare, or government sectors. Instead, they want us to think in terms of the whole.

Their global vision sees, for example, the auto industry working with the other sectors, not merely to advance their vehicles, but also to solve energy crises, climate change, and food shortages.

Do not misunderstand me. There is a time and place for looking at the big picture. However, when you begin with the wrong worldview, the big picture will be skewed. As the WEF seeks to unite our world's industries and economies, we see the stage being set for the Bible end times scenario to easily emerge.

Further, the WEF is in lockstep with the U.N. and its 2030 goals. In the same document, the WEF wrote, "Rather than using the ongoing crisis as a pretext to forego policies that support the transition to more sustainable energy sources, this moment should be utilized to develop more ambitious, comprehensive, and sustainable infrastructure investment plans that help the world to meet the 2030 targets."

---

27 World Economic Forum. https://www.weforum.org/events/world-economic-forum-annual-meeting-2023/about/meeting-overview

Rise of the One-World Mind

Translation: the crises we face may tempt us to stop pursuing the 2030 Agenda. However, the WEF sees this as an opportunity to push toward these goals more ambitiously than ever before. As we approach the year 2030, we will see much stronger efforts from the likes of the WEF and the U.N. to push us to a one-world system. I am not putting words in their mouths because they have said it themselves.

To solve every world problem, the WEF finds a globally centered solution. This follows perfectly with what the Bible teaches about the one-world economy during the Great Tribulation. While the WEF believes it is doing what is best for the world, they are ultimately setting the stage for the end-times rule of the Antichrist.

Digital Payment Systems

Aiding the move to a cashless society are breakthrough digital payment systems that connect your biometric information to your bank account.

Now you can pay with your palm thanks to Amazon One. How does this system work? A unit about the size of a retail card reader uses contactless biometric technology to scan the palm of your hand to collect your payment and connect with your retail rewards.

Amazon marketers are selling its added convenience with messaging like, "No more wallets needed. All you need is yourself. Your unique palm cannot be used by anyone else." They also tout a truly contactless payment option. Just hold your hand over the scanner and you are done.

How do they connect your palm to your bank account? You have to sign up using your Amazon account and then visit a location that has the Amazon One payment option to finish enrolling in person by scanning your palm. Once the system has registered your palm scan, you can use the palm scanner wherever it is available.

What is Amazon's long-term goal with this system? According to the official website for this venture, one.amazon.com, "Our goal is to unlock your world by giving you the freedom to pay, enter, and identify with nothing but your palm." Do you see how this goes far beyond another payment option at retailers? If you want to enter certain places, you must scan your palm. If you are asked to verify your identity, you must scan your palm.

Whether they realize it, this fits right into Bible prophecy during the Great Tribulation period. Revelation 13:16-17 describes the one-world economy under the Antichrist: "And he causeth all, both small and great, rich and poor, free and bond, to receive a mark in their right hand, or in their foreheads: And that no man might buy or sell, save he that had the mark, or the name of the beast, or the number of his name."

The phrase "mark in their right hand, or in their foreheads" receives a lot of attention. Over the last few years, many Bible prophecy teachers consider the little word "in" to refer to a microchip surgically inserted under the skin. While microchipping everyone certainly could happen down the road, the word "in" can also be translated as "on" and "upon." The King James Version translates this Greek word as "on" 196 times and as "in" 120 times.

It does not violate the context of Revelation 13:16 to understand "in" as "on." Therefore, in maintaining faithful biblical application of this verse, the mark of the beast does not have to be a physically implanted device. Amazon's palm pay technology requires no surgery or expensive medical devices, yet it carries out the same digital payment purpose as the chip technology.

Amazon is not alone in developing biometric payment systems. J.P. Morgan Payments began a pilot program in 2023 to test palm and facial recognition payment systems. They estimate global biometric payments to reach $5.8 trillion and 3 billion users by 2026, according to their research.[28] The technology is here to pay with your face or hand.

Amazon also has a technology called "Just Walk Out." Enter the store by scanning your hand with the Amazon One device, grab what you want, and just walk out. A system of cameras and shelf sensors monitors what the customer pulls off the shelf as they shop. If they change their mind and put something back on the shelf, the system recognizes that as well.

Large venues and stadiums are adding facial recognition software to allow people to enter by simply scanning their faces. Your face is your ticket.

Currency exchange kiosks are available across Europe that use facial recognition software.

---

28 J.P. Morgan, Inc. (2023, March 23) "J.P. Morgan to pilot biometrics-based payments for merchants." J.P. Morgan, Inc. https://www.jpmorgan.com/solutions/treasury-payments/insights/biometrics-checkout-us-pilot#:~:text=Global%20biometric%20payments%20are%20expected,experience%20to%20enhance%20customer%20loyalty

Now you can scan your face to board a plane in select airports. This technology makes it quicker and easier for people to get through security. Facial recognition is also being developed to help nations ID their citizens and businesses manage their employees' time punches.

It is dizzying to wrap our minds around this, and we've just scratched the surface. Once again, I am not anti-technology. Our ministry utilizes a lot of technology in our various avenues of ministry. It is very helpful. However, it is easy to see how the stage is being set for the biblical scenes that unfold during the Great Tribulation. Now is the time to get right with Jesus and walk closely with Him.

The Antichrist can take advantage of this kind of technology as he forces everyone to register their palm and facial recognition if they want to pay for anything, enter anywhere, and verify their identity.

ESG Scores and the One-World Economy

Have you wondered why corporations buy into the woke virtues of our day? I have heard several Christians ask, "Why can't they just stay neutral?" "Why do they pick sides?" ESG scores have a lot to do with it.

"What is an ESG score?" you might ask. ESG stands for environmental, social, and governance. "Environmental" scores describe how a company treats our environment. "Social" scores describe how a company treats people. "Governance" scores describe how well a company polices itself.

This basic understanding does not reveal the subjective nature of these scores. We must learn to ask important questions like, "Who determines what qualifies as a good ESG score? Who creates the categories and formulas to determine a good score? Who determines which values are more desirable than others?"

For example, should a restaurant chain receive a higher or lower environmental score if they still use plastic drinking straws? Should a company receive a higher or lower social score based on diversity and inclusivity? Should a company receive a higher or lower governance score if they donate money to politically conservative organizations? Someone has to answer these and many other questions to provide an ESG score for a company.

So, why are ESG scores important? Why do companies care about them in the first place? Major investment companies like BlackRock want the businesses they invest in to share similar corporate values. Thus, investment groups have put greater emphasis on ESG scores than mere profit performance. If companies want investment dollars, they must first achieve a high enough ESG score to prove they are worthy of the investment.

The investment firms are like a man holding a treat for his dog. If the dog does the trick the owner demands, then the dog gets the treat. No trick, no treat. The man holds all the power. Bad ESG scores equal no investment. The investment company holds all the power. If a company does not comply with the investment firm's ESG demands, then it will not receive investment dollars from that investment group.

This brings us back to the original question, "Why don't companies remain neutral on social issues?" It is because the investment companies will not allow them to remain neutral. Businesses are forced to align their corporate values with the investment firm or risk losing critical funds that can keep them afloat in an uncertain economy.

Let me show you some examples of how this happens in the corporate world. One of the key factors certain investors look for is a high score on the Human Rights Campaign's Corporate Equality Index. The campaign's website says this index is "the national benchmarking tool on corporate policies, practices and benefits pertinent to lesbian, gay, bisexual, transgender and queer employees." Out of the top 20 Fortune 500 companies, fifteen scored a perfect 100 on this index including Walmart, Amazon, Apple, CVS Health, Google, AT&T, and Verizon in 2023.

To get a perfect 100 score on the Human Rights Campaign's Index, companies must offer inclusive workforce protections for sexual orientation and gender identity. They must also offer inclusive benefits to fund items like transgender-inclusive health insurance. Further, the companies must actively engage and support the LGBTQ+ community through philanthropic giving.

But if you want to get a perfect 100 score, you must go a step further. Corporations could be tempted to play both sides with their charitable donations, so the Human Rights Campaign will not give a perfect 100 score to any company that donates to a non-religious organization with a written policy in opposition to the LGBTQ+ cause. All fifteen of the top 20 Fortune 500 companies who received a perfect 100 score are following these values.

Biblically conservative Christians have long championed Chick-fil-A as a restaurant chain led by biblical values. However, in 2012, they stopped supporting a plethora of Christian organizations. In 2019, they dropped their support of the two faith-based groups that survived their 2012 cuts—the Salvation Army and Fellowship of Christian Athletes. They began giving donations to groups with pro-LGBTQ+ stances. In 2021, the corporation hired a vice president of diversity, equity, and inclusion.

As of this writing, Chick-fil-A is not listed on the Human Rights Campaign Index. However, its corporate actions seem like they are actively seeking a higher ESG score. Chick-fil-A uses a franchise model, so each owner-operator may or may not hold these corporate values.

How do ESG scores tie into a one-world economy? Corporations are already conditioned to align their values with investment companies. As the world moves to a CBDC and a global economy, corporations will be forced to align if they want to survive. If individuals will be pressured by a CBDC, can you imagine what a company will undergo? It will be impossible to do business in a one-world system without aligning with the powers that be.

A common thread we see in this chapter is a prevailing attitude of "get on board with us, or else." The U.N. will stop at nothing to see its Agenda 2030 come to fruition. The WEF conditions our world to pursue globalism. Investment companies use ESG scores to force businesses to align. We have the technology to make the digital switch to a cashless economy.

The stage is set for a one-world economy to emerge. The biblical Great Tribulation prophecies will be a reality. This is not speculation. I have shared facts and information about what is happening in our world today.

The last section of this book is dedicated to solutions. We need to prepare for what is coming. In light of all this information, we need to know how to live in today's world. Before we launch into that discussion, we need to understand the rise of the one-world worship mindset and the role AI plays in the rise of the one-world mind.

RISE OF THE ONE-WORLD WORSHIP MINDSET

The term "one-world worship" refers to the global spiritual system the world will unite under during the Great Tribulation. Some refer to this as the "one-world religion," however, the world is experiencing a decline in religion. People prefer to be called spiritual instead of religious, as detailed in this chapter's section called "Hallmarks of One-World Worship." While many people would not call themselves religious, everyone worships something or someone. The rising trend in spirituality today is rooted in paganism and fulfilling the desires of self.

Make no mistake, our world is moving in this direction. I will show you information that backs up this claim. The best information I can start with is Scripture. Bible prophecy is clear. There will be a one-world system of worship during the Great Tribulation.

One-world worship will motivate the move to a one-world economy. Worship is the glue that holds the one-world economy and government together during the Great Tribulation.

How can I make such a claim? Consider Revelation 13. Three figures lead blasphemous worship during the Great Tribulation—the dragon (identified as Satan in Revelation 12), the beast from the sea, and the beast from the Earth.

Empowered by Satan, the beast from the sea rises to prominence among a coalition of rulers (Rev. 13:1-2; Dan. 7:7-8). The similarity between Daniel's prophecy of the Roman Empire and the description in Revelation 13 seems to indicate a revived Roman Empire during the Great Tribulation with this beast as its leader.

Truly, the revived Roman Empire combines the symbolism of all four kingdoms described in Daniel's vision (Rev. 13:1-2; Dan. 7:1-8). Daniel saw a lion (Babylon), a bear (Medo-Persia), a leopard (Greece), and a ten-horned beast (Rome). John's beast from the sea looks like a leopard with the feet of a bear and the mouth of a lion. This beast has seven heads and ten horns and is fueled by the dragon, Satan.

One of the seven heads is mortally wounded by a sword (Rev. 13:3,14). It appears to the world this wound is fatal but this person, symbolized by a head, recovers in a seemingly miraculous fashion.

Someone dies and comes back to life. Where have we heard that before? Yes, Jesus! That is one of the reasons why this beast empowered by Satan is called the Antichrist. He is a Messianic imposter who deceives the world.

The world is shocked at the news of his sudden recovery and begins to worship Satan and the Antichrist (Rev. 13:3-4). The saying will be, "Who is like unto the beast? who is able to make war with him?" (Rev. 13:4).

The fact that the Antichrist is mortally wounded by a sword and is worshiped based on his apparent indestructibility tells us he has enemies. The world is not united when he rises to power.

This apparent resurrection becomes a catalyst for his rise to authority over the whole world (Rev. 13:5-7). But the Bible is clear, this is all deception. We read, "whose coming is after the working of Satan with all power and signs and lying wonders" (2 Thess. 2:9).

The Antichrist uses his fake resurrection to claim to be God. Paul warned about the Antichrist's deception by telling us, "Who opposeth and exalteth himself above all that is called God, or that is worshipped; so that he as God sitteth in the temple of God, showing himself that he is God" (2 Thess. 2:4).

John informs us the Antichrist's campaign will be successful for 42 months. "And he opened his mouth in blasphemy against God, to blaspheme his name, and his tabernacle, and them that dwell in heaven. And it was given unto him to make war with the saints, and to overcome them: and power was given him over all kindreds, and tongues, and nations" (Rev. 13:6-7).

The whole unbelieving world will be convinced he has supernatural powers. Only those who have called upon Jesus for salvation during the Great Tribulation will oppose worshiping the Antichrist. "And all that dwell upon the earth shall worship him, whose names are not written in the book of life of the Lamb slain from the foundation of the world" (Rev. 13:8).

If that is not bad enough, a second beast will come up from out of the Earth with "two horns like a lamb, and he spake as a dragon" (Rev. 13:11). Once again, this imagery points to great deception. He appears as gentle as a lamb, yet is filled with Satan.

With the emergence of this figure, the unholy trinity is complete. Satan is an imposter of the Father, the Antichrist is an imposter of Jesus, and this False Prophet is an imposter of the Holy Spirit. The Antichrist becomes the political figurehead of the Great Tribulation and the False Prophet becomes the religious figurehead.

The False Prophet will deceive the world through lying signs and wonders equal to the Antichrist. But, instead of receiving worship himself, he will point people to the Antichrist. "And he exerciseth all the power of the first beast before him, and causeth the earth and them which dwell therein to worship the first beast, whose deadly wound was healed" (Rev. 13:12). Do you see how diabolically self-abasing this false Holy Spirit will appear to be?

Do you recall Elijah versus the false prophets of Baal upon Mount Carmel (1 Kings 18)? Elijah challenged them to ask their god to send fire down from heaven upon the sacrificial altar. Hundreds of false prophets did everything they could for hours, but nothing happened. Elijah prayed a short prayer and the fire of God fell from heaven and obliterated the sacrificial altar.

The False Prophet will imitate Elijah's miracle. "And he doeth great wonders, so that he maketh fire come down from heaven on the earth in the sight of men" (Rev. 13:13).

The world will attribute this miracle to the divine. They will buy into this deceitful sign. He will use this acceptance to request them to, "make an image to the beast, which had the wound by a sword, and did live" (Rev. 13:14). Once more, the False Prophet will deflect worship to the Antichrist with an air of false humility.

The world will build this idolatrous image, then the False Prophet will do the unthinkable. "And he had power to give life unto the image of the beast, that the image of the beast should both speak, and cause that as many as would not worship the image of the beast should be killed" (Rev. 13:15).

The False Prophet gives life to this image of the beast in such a way that it can speak and identify who worships the image of the beast and who does not. Those who refuse to worship this image of the beast will be killed.

I think this could be either an active or passive killing. If it is an active killing, the image of the beast would have the capability to identify and command the killing. Concentration camps could return.

However, it could also be a passive killing by simply cutting off all resources to those who refuse to worship. Recall what I shared in the last chapter. With a digital one-world economy in place, this image of the beast could shut off access to money to make it impossible to buy and sell. Combine that with the devastation to the planet during the Great Tribulation, and the choice becomes either worship or die through starvation, disease, or other passive means.

A few short years ago, it was difficult to imagine how the False Prophet could give this kind of "life" to an image. How could an image speak? How could an image control people? With the exponential capabilities of artificial intelligence, the technology is here for this to be a reality. It is not so far-fetched, is it?

The next three verses that end Revelation 13 describe the one-world economy ushered in by the False Prophet by enforcing the mark of the beast (Rev. 13:16-18). I explained those verses in the last chapter so I will not rehash that here. But please do not miss the connection between worship, the government, and the economy during the Great Tribulation. It is all tied together in Bible prophecy.

The Antichrist will not be a mere political ruler. He will claim to be divine and worship will be demanded. Consider again 2 Thessalonians 2:4, "Who opposeth and exalteth himself above all that is called God, or that is worshipped; so that he as God sitteth in the temple of God, showing himself that he is God."

The Antichrist will seek to unite the world in worship by pointing out the flaws of all the other world religions and offering himself as the solution. Why do I say that? Notice the first line of this verse – he will oppose anything called "God" and will exalt himself above all other objects of worship.

The fact that he will sit in the temple of God can be both literal and symbolic. It could be literal if his image occupies the physical future temple in Jerusalem during the Great Tribulation. It can also be symbolic in that each person will place the Antichrist in the position only the one true God should occupy in their lives. This is not an either-or proposition. It could prove to be both-and.[29]

The fact remains the coming one-world government and economy will be glued together by one-world worship during the Great Tribulation. How do we see this taking shape in our world today?

---

29 For detailed information on the future Millennial Temple in Jerusalem, consult Shipman, Lonnie. *Treasure and the Coming Temple of God* (Oklahoma City, OK: Beacon Street Press, 2023).

One-World Worship Rising

People are already discussing how AI could be used to create a religious book. For example, Professor Yuval Noah Harari, who has ties to the WEF, said in an interview that AI could be used to write a new Bible since it is the first technology that can generate ideas of its own.[30] He added, "Throughout history, religions dreamt about having a book written by a super-human intelligence, by a non-human entity. Every religion claims, 'Our book – all the other books of the other religions, they – humans wrote them, but our book, no, no, no, no, no, it came from some super-human intelligence.' In a few years, there might be religions that are actually correct. That – just think about a religion whose holy book is written by an AI. That could be a reality in a few years."[31]

Do you remember what Revelation 13:5 said? The Antichrist will continue his rule for 42 months, which appears to begin at the midpoint of the 7-year-long Great Tribulation. So, when Harari says an AI religious text could be a reality in a few years, we know we are standing on the threshold. Technologically speaking, the Great Tribulation could begin today.

This propels us into a larger discussion of the timing of the rapture of the church. However, permit me to put that off for a few chapters. Suffice it to say, I believe the Bible teaches the imminence of the rapture. In other words, the rapture of the church could happen at any moment. We do not need to see AI advance before the rapture can occur, but the fact that the technology is available right now to make every prophecy a reality confirms just how close we are.

Are there other signposts that point to one-world worship? In America and around the world are properties devoted to worshiping as one, sometimes called "interfaith centers." In Omaha, Nebraska, sits the Tri-Faith Commons which houses a Jewish synagogue, a Muslim mosque and a Christian church. This Tri-Faith Center is all linked together by a circular bridge they call "Abraham's Bridge."[32] Get this, according to their website, Abraham's Bridge runs over Hell's Creek. Other online listings refer to this as "Hell Creek," which runs through part of Omaha.[33] You cannot make this stuff up!

---

30 Yuval Noah Harari. (2023, June 6) "Humanity is not that simple – Yuval Noah Harari & Pedro Pinto," YouTube. (6:20-8:45). https://www.youtube.com/watch?v=4hIlDiVDww4&t=1s.

31 Ibid.

32 Tri-Faith Initiative. (Accessed 2023, July 25) "Abraham's Bridge." https://www.trifaith.org/thecommons/abrahams-bridge/

33 For example, maps.google.com lists it as "Hell Creek," as do numerous other websites.

In 2023, the Abrahamic Family House opened in Abu Dhabi. Out of the Middle Eastern desert, this property rose with a Muslim mosque, Jewish synagogue, and Roman Catholic church connected with other spaces for people of all faiths to worship. To have this kind of property in a Muslim-majority nation speaks loudly about where worship is heading.

Hallmarks of One-World Worship

There are specific hallmarks that make these properties possible. These hallmarks set the stage for a global system of worship during the Great Tribulation. The unholy trinity could manipulate people along these lines and then bring in their one-world system of worship as the Bible foretells.

First, one-world religion emphasizes a works-based religious system. To get to this stage, what you do must be more important than what you believe. Doctrine must be ignored in the pursuit of good works. The message becomes "What brings us together is more important than our differences."

Secondly, one-world religion emphasizes human-centered worship. The message is, "Follow your heart. Find your truth." Worship becomes a means to self-fulfillment. Thus, it becomes more about finding yourself than finding the one true God.

Thirdly, one-world religion emphasizes saving humanity and the planet. It focuses more on making this a better world to live in than on preparing for eternity. Messages, songs, and other acts of public worship will focus on the here and now instead of the transcendent.

Fourthly, one-world religion emphasizes spirituality over religion. The term "religion" carries some negative baggage with it in modern times. It seems like a restrictive system under the authority of power-hungry people. However, the term "spiritual" seems very positive and inclusive. This term will be used more and more as one-world worship emerges. Thus, personal feelings hold more weight than faith in the one true God. It pairs well with the postmodern thought of our day that will never tell anyone they are wrong for their spiritual beliefs.

Lastly, one-world religion emphasizes a higher power over the one true God. Relativistic postmodernism preaches truth is in the eye of the beholder. Just like "spiritual" versus "religious," "higher power" seems more accepting in modern thought. Thus, it values relativistic subjective perspectives over absolute truth. "You have your higher power, I have mine," goes the line, "Let's set aside our differences and focus on making this world a better place to live."

These mindsets toward worship are growing as the years roll by. Even worship leaders have promoted a globalist agenda. By "worship leaders" I do not mean those who lead music at church on Sundays. I am talking about Protestant church leaders.

Did you hear what these Protestant church leaders envisioned to bring about world peace? They asked for a world government of delegated powers. They also called for worldwide freedom of immigration, a "democratically controlled" international bank, and "a universal system of money."

Further, they reasoned that many of the duties performed by local and national governments, "can now be effectively carried out only by international authority."

What was the ultimate goal these Protestant church leaders envisioned? "A duly constituted world government of delegated powers: an international legislative body, an international court with adequate jurisdiction, international administrative bodies with necessary powers, and adequate international police forces and provision for enforcing its worldwide economic authority."

When was this written? Who are these church leaders? Why haven't we heard about this? You are probably asking lots of questions about this statement from Protestant church leaders. I have held you in suspense long enough.

TIME magazine published this story on March 16, 1942. Yes, the move to globalism is not new and infiltrated the Protestant church many years ago.

This TIME magazine article is titled, "Religion: American Malvern."[34] It describes a meeting of what was then called the "Federal Council of Churches," now known as the "National Council of Churches." It was mind-blowing to me when I first realized how far back the one-world mindset goes in the American Protestant church.

Ultimately, the one-world worship is rooted in pride. Humanity puffs itself up thinking we can accomplish anything we set our minds to. Pride has plagued us since the beginning.

The tower of Babel stood as a symbol of man's prideful ability to bridge the gap between heaven and Earth (Gen. 11:1-9). The people united with one language in open rebellion against God. So too the unholy trinity will usher in a

---

34 TIME. (1942, March 16) "Religion: American Malvern." https://content.time.com/time/subscriber/article/0,33009,801396,00.html

one-world system in open rebellion against God. Just as God came down upon Babel in judgment, so too the Second Coming will dismantle the one-world system of the Great Tribulation.

As we observe the rise of the one-world mind all around us today, we see the pitfall of pride taking hold of the powerful. They think that they are accomplishing their agenda right here, right now. However, God's kingdom is advancing and His prophetic plan for the ages is unfolding exactly as He said.

God has promised to put down the proud on the Day of the Lord. "And I will punish the world for their evil, and the wicked for their iniquity; and I will cause the arrogancy of the proud to cease, and will lay low the haughtiness of the terrible" (Isa. 13:11).

When Jesus returns to Earth in his Second Coming, the unholy trinity will be disbanded forever. "And the beast was taken, and with him the false prophet that wrought miracles before him, with which he deceived them that had received the mark of the beast, and them that worshipped his image. These both were cast alive into a lake of fire burning with brimstone" (Rev. 19:20).

Satan's counterfeit lasts a few short years and ends with death and defeat, but God's kingdom is forever and His followers will praise Him forever!

Perhaps you can tell how anxious I am to share some solutions with you. We are getting there, I promise. We need to expose some more potential road hazards before we move on to a roadmap to help us navigate the rise of the one-world mind.

RISE OF ARTIFICIAL INTELLIGENCE

"Open the pod bay doors, HAL."

"I'm sorry, Dave. I'm afraid I can't do that."

In this well-known interaction from the 1968 movie "2001: A Space Odyssey," Dave the astronaut is denied reentry into the spaceship by the computer system named HAL. Artificial technology took control of the ship to save itself from the astronauts who decided to destroy this technology that had a mind of its own.

From "Terminator" to "The Matrix," sci-fi movies cause us to imagine a world where technology transforms life as we know it. When these movies first hit theaters, they were very popular in part because the scenarios were so far-fetched at the time. However, with the rise of AI, fiction does not seem so far away.

AI is an infant. Before we get sucked in by the "ooh, shiny new stuff" vibes, we must consider the potential harms presented by AI. Before you write me off as a crotchety technology hater, consider the fact that tech giants like Elon Musk and Sam Altman, co-founder of OpenAI, warn us to proceed with caution.

Here is a sentence I never thought I would write: What does the pope riding a motorcycle through a crowded city street and Donald Trump handcuffed by a swarm of police officers have in common? Both images appeared very realistic but they were created with AI art in 2022.

Remember, technology is a tool. AI art can be used for good and helpful purposes but it can also be used to deceive others.

Anyone with an internet connection can use AI art tools. Some AI art generators take basic keywords you input and create an image based on the terms you selected. For example, I could input "lion in the desert, high detail, photo-realistic," and poof! My image is generated and available for my use. Since this technology is so new, it makes mistakes, so you better count how many legs that lion has.

There are free apps available that will take photos you upload from your tablet or mobile device and apply AI filters in a variety of styles. People are finding hours of entertainment by playing around with silly word combinations or funny images.

However, these image generators have also been applied in less-than-wholesome ways. Creating fake images of famous persons has blurred the lines between fact and fiction and makes the masses think, "Did this really happen?" Are we going to have to ask that question every time we see images in the future?

Tech giants like Google are considering measures to label fake AI-generated images across the internet so people can tell what is real and what is fake. This could open a whole new can of worms with the debate over internet control.

The creators of AI art generators have banned certain search terms from being used to curb an explosion of explicit content and gore.

Beyond depravity, one of the greatest risks with AI art generators is the power to deceive. Seeing is no longer believing. Images could be used to defend a lie and deceive the world. Could the Antichrist utilize an AI art generator to spread his propaganda and put down his adversaries?

Art is far from the only capability of AI Chat-bots like ChatGPT can create entire books based on a few short prompts from a user. Soon after this AI software was launched, educators scrambled to build AI software detectors so students could not cheat on writing assignments.

If students rely on technology like this to complete their writing assignments, it will seriously harm their reasoning skills and ability to communicate with others. "There goes the crotchety man again," you may be thinking. Let me give you a personal example to explain why I know this will happen.

The majority of my elementary, middle, and high school years were in the 1990s. Now you're thinking, "Wow, crotchety and old!" When I turned 16 years old and started driving, I got my first cell phone. It was about the size of a brick and you needed a phone book to go with it because it could not store any numbers.

In math class, a constant complaint from my classmates was, "Why can't we use a calculator?" My teachers wanted us to be able to solve simple math equations with our minds. They were training our brains to think correctly. While I was certainly in the pro-calculator crowd at the time, today I see the wisdom in my math teachers' approach.

As an adult, I became reliant upon calculators to do my basic math quickly and accurately. It has severely slowed down my ability to do simple math. This reliance on technology has changed the way I think. How do I know? When I need to do math, my first thought is to open my phone's calculator.

Future generations will use AI text generators much like I use a calculator, to the detriment of communication skills. Why should anyone spend hours combing through research materials and organizing an outline when you can have a robust research project written in mere minutes with AI? Critical thinking skills will greatly diminish as a result.

Educators are correct to be concerned about students' reliance on AI text generators. I am convinced the church should be concerned about this too.

In June 2023, AI text generator software ChatGPT was used to create a church service for about 300 congregants in Germany. A large screen over the altar displayed digital human avatars speaking the words generated by ChatGPT, including a 40-minute sermon.

What happens to a body of believers when the pastors begin to shortcut their sermon preparation with ChatGPT? Pastors are pressed for time as it is. I fear that preachers will become more reliant on technology and less adept at accurately handling the Word of God. Just as my calculator changed my math instincts, will text generators change our sermon preparation instincts? If it does, it will be to the detriment of Christ's church.

Consider Paul's charge to Timothy. "I charge thee therefore before God, and the Lord Jesus Christ, who shall judge the quick and the dead at his appearing and his kingdom; Preach the Word; be instant in season, out of season; reprove, rebuke, exhort with all longsuffering and doctrine" (2 Tim. 4:1-2).

Preachers will stand before God and give account for how they handled God's Word. We must continue to grow in our knowledge of God through His Word and faithfully proclaim it to others. Of all the things a pastor can shortcut, time spent in God's Word must not be one of them.

Why did Paul issue such a strong charge to Timothy? The next two verses explain. "For the time will come when they will not endure sound doctrine; but after their own lusts shall they heap to themselves teachers, having itching ears; And they shall turn away their ears from the truth, and shall be turned unto fables" (2 Tim. 4:3-4).

While false teachers have plagued the church since it began, the rise of AI could scratch a lot of itching ears by telling folks what they want to hear instead of what they need to hear from God's Word. Just enter a few keywords, and poof, out comes your spiritual lesson for the day according to your liking. It could become a major detriment to discipleship and the role of the Holy Spirit in the life of the church.

Once more, I am not anti-technology. I use Bible study software programs every day. What used to take minutes to find the right book and flip to the right page now takes mere seconds. I love it! It is a major time saver.

I can remember in my early days of seminary and ministry before I invested in a good Bible study software program, I would have a whole table full of books with paper and napkins stuffed here and there to mark my places. Now I can carry a whole library of Bible study resources in my pocket thanks to this growing technology.

Our ministry seeks to utilize any technology we can muster to help us spread God's truth as far and as wide as possible. Without our cutting-edge technology, this book would not exist and would not look as great as it does.

I am simply urging us to proceed with caution as we enter the world of AI. If it can be used as a tool to advance the truth, by all means, use it but do not let the tool become a crutch.

Beyond AI art and text, voice generators are quickly gaining popularity. Soon the days of the obviously computerized voice will be over. These voice generators take the text you type into it and give it a voice.

Some AI voice generators can simulate anyone's voice with just a few seconds of sample audio. Simply provide the AI voice generator with enough sample audio from the person's voice you wish to copy, and it can mimic their voice with your custom text.

People will have fun playing with this technology. Imagine some of your favorite celebrities speaking your text through these powerful AI generators. This could provide endless hours of entertainment. Kids, please do not prank Grandma! Sorry, the dad in me had to come out.

One of the great benefits of this technology is that text can be instantly translated into multiple languages. This could make it much easier to spread God's truth around the world in multiple languages. Potentially, text from this book could be inputted into an AI voice generator so that people who cannot read English could hear it in their native language. That is mind-blowing to consider!

While this technology has the potential for great good, we must also consider the potential for harm. Our ministry has been on the radio for 90 years. Someone could upload a sample of any of our hosts' or guests' voices then type in any text they want it to say, and out it comes.

Technology is here to literally put words in our mouths. AI voice generators could be used to ruin careers, sway elections, impact courtroom evidence, and transform how we live.

As we see AI move from infancy to adulthood, we must not rush to judgment when we see or hear something unexpected from a trusted voice. Sadly, our culture already rushes to judgment on everything. People on social media get a lot of exercise through their favorite sport – jumping to conclusions. We must guard against this as AI develops because we might see and hear things that simply are not true.

I hope you have picked up on the fact that I have attempted to be fair and optimistic about some of the positive aspects of AI. I haven't held back my concerns. Yet there is one aspect of AI that I have not touched on.

AI is developing rapidly and it is constantly "learning." I put "learning" in quotes because true learning is a capacity only living beings can accomplish. AI processes mountains of data and then uses that information to produce content. It can read a world full of books and harness all the information they contain. AI could quickly become the go-to expert in all fields of education.

One of the key questions I have asked throughout this book is, "What happens when this tool falls into the wrong hands?" During the Great Tribulation, could the Antichrist and his cohorts use AI to quickly "learn" and catalog everything about you? Every picture you take, every post you make on social media, every item you buy with digital currency, every calorie you consume, and every place you go could be monitored and controlled through future AI technology.

The likes of Yuval Noah Harari and Klaus Schwab warn of a coming technological revolution like the world has never seen. Could AI replace an entire workforce and eliminate the need for millions of jobs? Harari refers to this coming storm as the creation of a "useless class."[35]

---

35 Carnegie Council for Ethics in International Affairs. (Accessed 2023, July 29) "Yuval Noah Harari: Workplace Automation & the 'Useless Class.'" YouTube. https://www.youtube.com/watch?v=OMDlfNWM1fA

He argues that during previous industrial revolutions, workers were able to move from one industry to another with relative ease. For example, a farmer replaced by technological innovations could get a job on an assembly line in Detroit. When technology replaced people on assembly lines, people could get a job in retail. Now technology is replacing people in retail.

Where will the next opportunity come? People will be forced to get specialized training in a new field because technology is eliminating most of the low-skill jobs. What about those without access to education in developing countries? These people will be left on the outside of the job market with no place to go. These are the people Harari refers to as the "useless class." There will be zero jobs available for them because AI and advanced technology will replace all the low-skill jobs.

What is the solution to this approaching crisis? Harari praises countries that have high taxes and state-run welfare programs to provide for the people. But what happens when developing countries that are already struggling are no longer able to provide for their citizens?

I think this explains why the U.N. is pushing so hard for its Agenda 2030 and why it offers a Marxist solution for global problems. Further, a borderless world in which we all "cooperate" (remember the new definition of that term) could be the solution offered to help starving people in failing countries.

A one-world government and economy will be the solution the world needs when the job market makes this dramatic shift. If the world is one, the government can give essentials like food and clean water to everyone around the world so that no one goes hungry. Cooperation will replace competition so that no one gets left behind. Education will give people all over the world access to better jobs.

Please do not misunderstand me. I am not proposing a one-world solution. I am trying to get you to see the mindset that is growing in our world today. The areas we have considered thus far are not individual entities. They are all a cohesive whole. That is why I included this chapter on technology. What was once deemed impossible is on the verge of existence because of these pioneer technologies.

Do you see how easy it will be for the world to buy into the "Ooh, shiny new stuff" vibes? The globalist solutions will make logical sense to the majority of Earth's population during the Great Tribulation.

In Revelation 13, the one-world government, economy, and worship all flow seamlessly together. Technology will enable them to accomplish their global goals. While people will go along with the shiny new stuff at first, they will soon realize the horrible downside.

The world's desires will quickly turn into a nightmare as people are forced to comply with the demands of the Antichrist and False Prophet as they take control and demand worship.

If you are a follower of Jesus, this should not scare you because we will be in heaven during the Great Tribulation. However, those alive on Earth during this time will experience all these things. We must use the time we have right now to prepare ourselves for eternity. If your life on Earth would end today, do you know where you will spend eternity?

Before we move toward solutions, we need to come face to face with a prevalent attitude that powers the rise of the one-world mind – malignant narcissism. That sounds like a nasty virus, doesn't it? Don't worry. It is 100% curable.

CURING MALIGNANT NARCISSISM

Imagine you are a 30-something-year-old parent driving down the road one lazy summer Saturday with the windows down and the radio on. Your kids are in the backseat enjoying the breeze and the bright sunshine. As you scan the radio signals, you land on a classic hits station playing Bon Jovi.

He's reaching the chorus of his hit song and you sing it loud and proud, "It's my life / It's now or never / I ain't gonna live forever / I just want to live while I'm alive / It's my life / My heart is like an open highway / Like Frankie said "I did it my way" / I just wanna live while I'm alive / It's my life."

Thoroughly embarrassed by your performance, one of your kids tries her best to change the station as fast as possible from the backseat.

It lands on a classic station playing the elegant strains of Frank Sinatra. "And more, much more / I did it, I did it my way," he exclaims. Your attempts to emulate the crooner redouble the efforts of your kids to change the station yet again.

This time it lands on a Taylor Swift song. Which one? It doesn't matter because they all sound the same. You hit the search button swifter than Taylor could get out the words about moving on from that guy who dumped her.

It happens to land on a Christian station playing a positive song. "Don't lose heart / Don't you dare let go / I've been where you are / You are not alone / I know it gets dark / I know it gets hard / But we're gonna make it home / So don't lose heart."

Your kids ask, "What does 'make it home' mean?" About that time, you pull into your driveway, turn off the car, and facetiously tell your kids, "We made it home!"

Did you realize these songs reveal the rise of the last-day mindset?

The Bible tells us, "This know also, that in the last days perilous times shall come. For men shall be lovers of their own selves" (2 Tim. 3:1-2a).

This brings us to the curious title of this chapter, "curing malignant narcissism." Based on these song lyrics, it's clear that we live in a time when people know how to love themselves.

That's the common thread woven in each of these songs. "It's my life." "I did it my way." Even some Christian songs promote a human-centered solution to problems too big for us to solve without God.

Our me-centered world preaches, "Look within yourself. You have the power within you to accomplish your dreams. Choose you." When we buy into this message, we create a new god.

I am convinced the number one "god" in America is self. We do what we want to do when we want to do it. We don't like it when people tell us we're wrong because we've decided we're right. We live to pursue our desires and find what makes us happy. The result of our humanistic worship is narcissism – a selfish me-first mindset.

Narcissism is our perfume of choice. Its scent is noticeable to all those around us.

Have you ever heard about going "nose blind?" That is what happens when we get used to smelling a certain scent so long that our nose adapts to it and we no longer smell the scent.

The fact is, we have gone nose blind to our narcissism and it is reaching pandemic proportions. "Malignant" simply refers to the fast-spreading nature of this worldview virus.

The Apostle Paul, who wrote the words of 2 Timothy 3, wakes up our noses from blindness by showering us with the ingredients from which the nauseous stench of narcissism is created. I pray as we walk through these ingredients, your nose will recognize malignant narcissism for the putrid stench it is. I pray you will recognize the idolatry inherent in malignant narcissism.

Just so you know I'm not trying to be a negative Nancy or Debbie downer, I follow the text of 2 Timothy to the potent cure it provides for malignant narcissism. So, hang with me as we expose the virus before explaining the cure.

Walk with me through 5 steps to curing malignant narcissism mentioned in this important chapter.

Step 1 — Recognize Error

We cannot move to healing and authentic wholeness until we first recognize that something is wrong, something is missing. That is why step one in the Bible's cure for malignant narcissism is to recognize error. This error will create difficult times for people who fall for it.

Why will difficult times come in the last days? Paul's list of ingredients points to one common source – self. Paul began his list with, "For men shall be lovers of their own selves" (2 Tim. 3:2a). The list that follows explains what self-love looks like.

Before we examine each ingredient, consider the recipe for disaster that creates a house of worship I call the "Temple of Self:"

For men shall be lovers of their own selves, covetous, boasters, proud, blasphemers, disobedient to parents, unthankful, unholy, Without natural affection, trucebreakers, false accusers, incontinent, fierce, despisers of those that are good, Traitors, heady, high-minded, lovers of pleasures more than lovers of God; Having a form of godliness, but denying the power thereof: from such turn away (2 Tim. 3:2-5).

Following lovers of self, the next ingredient is being "covetous." Literally, this word means to be a "lover of silver." Materialism is the garb of the self's false god. It is not a sin to be wealthy or to have nice things. However, it becomes an idol when its pursuit fills our minds and hearts. When we make a top priority of getting, making, and maintaining our stuff, we have created an idol. We fill the Temple of Self with the stuff we love.

The next two ingredients are similar to each other – "boasters" and "proud." Boasting is the external revelation of an internal attitude of pride. Arrogance arises from our hearts and exits out of our mouths. The worship songs we sing in the Temple of Self extol our goodness and greatness.

When the object of worship becomes humanity, we become "blasphemers." The Temple of Self pushes out all other objects of worship. What do I mean? Even some who sit on church pews each Sunday say they worship Jesus as their God, yet their lives deny that claim when they live contrary to His truth and follow whatever they want instead. In so doing, their selfish actions reveal their true god is self, not Jesus. So, the malignant narcissist might pledge allegiance to Jesus, but when push comes to shove, the self conquers all other objects of worship.

In the Temple of Self, there is one commandment, "Do whatever pleases you." The narcissistic lifestyle is marked by pursuing our desires. The next ingredient is a natural consequence of that attitude – "disobedient to parents." Authority that seeks to hinder whatever pleases you must, therefore, be cast off, ignored, and rejected. "It's my life" after all, right?

The Temple of Self is an unthankful place. Think about it. Narcissism cares only about the self and uses others to gratify the self's desires. Gratitude comes from a heart that values others. Arrogance blinds gratefulness.

Self-worship is marked by "unholy" conduct. Since the self defines what is and is not called "holy," God's standard of holiness is tossed out of the Temple of Self. Thus, God's truth is replaced by what we call good.

The next ingredient is "without natural affection." In other words, this is someone who is hardhearted or unfeeling. They are callous toward the needs of others. When you worship at the Temple of Self, you have no time to notice the needs of others as you pursue your desires.

The god of self is not the forgiving sort. The walls of the Temple of Self are covered with a list of names of those who have wronged us and the transgressions they have committed against us. Judgment and revenge are stored up by the self until the moment it can be unleashed upon the offender. This is what is meant by the term "trucebreakers."

Since the self is not all-knowing or perfect, its vengeful spirit creates "false accusers." In an attempt to promote one's Temple of Self above another's, slanderous words become the weapon of choice.

When the slanderous arrows start to fly, self-control is lost. A hallmark of the Temple of Self is a total lack of self-control. "Live in the moment. Do what makes you happy. Follow your heart." These words become the message and mantra in the Temple of Self. These attitudes describe the ingredient "incontinent."

Linked to a lack of self-control, the next ingredient is "fierce." This speaks to a savage attitude that acts like a wild animal. It's the opposite of civilized behavior. The self pursues its desires with reckless abandon and leaves a trail of brokenness in its wake.

In the Temple of Self, morality is determined by the individual, not by an external standard such as God. Thus, a hatred for anything and anyone that

God and the Bible calls "good" permeates the mind in the Temple of Self. That's what is meant by the ingredient, "despisers of those that are good."

When your allegiance is only to yourself and no external standard, you have no problem being a traitor, the next ingredient mentioned. The Bible uses this same word when it describes how Judas Iscariot betrayed Jesus (Luke 6:16). It's difficult to admit that we might have an attitude similar to Judas Iscariot. The Scripture is clear. The end-times mindset will emulate Judas Iscariot's selfishness.

The next two ingredients are "heady" and "highminded." To be "heady" is to be rash, reckless, and thoughtless. To be "highminded" is to be conceited and extremely prideful. If all your thoughts are about yourself, you will have no time for others. Everyone will look out for themselves and their best interests. Christians like to say, "Put God first in all things." The Temple of Self has no problem with that since each person is a god unto themselves.

The next ingredient reveals the true object of worship in someone's life — "lovers of pleasures more than lovers of God." The Golden Rule in the Temple of Self is, "Pursue your desires." This humanistic religion preaches, "Find yourself by pursuing what makes you happy."

What if a married man with a wife and young kids decided he wanted to pursue what makes him happy, so he left his family behind to pursue his selfish desires? The Temple of Self should praise such a man for boldly following himself. However, I think worshipers at this Temple would have a nagging feeling that this is not right. Where would that thought come from? Would we call this man a good father for forgetting his kids to pursue his desires?

The Temple of Self preaches, "Forget those thoughts!" As we try to justify ourselves, we can't escape the feeling that this is just plain wrong.

The final ingredient in this recipe for disaster reveals a sinister side to the whole lot — "having a form of godliness but denying the power thereof." While posing to be a true follower of Jesus, lovers of self talk the talk but do not walk the walk. We can summarize this in one word: hypocrisy.

In giving this list, Paul addressed false teachers who would come into the church to deceive believers. His admonition to his readers was, "from such turn away" (2 Tim. 3:5). In other words, beware of these attitudes because they will lead you away from Jesus and deeper into false worship at the Temple of Self.

The deeper you go into self-worship, serious real-world consequences begin to appear.

It is no coincidence that as malignant narcissism rises in our day, mental health issues simultaneously reach epidemic proportions. Anxiety and depression numbers continue to rise in America. While several factors can contribute to anxiety and depression, the Temple of Self plays a significant role.

When people constantly hear messages like, "You are enough," or, "Find yourself by looking within," we come to believe we have the solution to all our problems within ourselves. What happens when we realize we do not? Anxiety and depression rise as our dreams shatter around us.

Graduation commencement speeches are peppered with statements like, "You have the power to go out and change the world!" Yet as graduates end their education and enter the marketplace, they eventually realize they aren't changing the world like they thought they would.

The god of self is a crushing tyrant. We claw to advance ourselves and to change the world. Yet life pushes us back down as we quickly realize everyone else is trying to go out and change the world into their image for what it should be.

There is no contentment or peace in this lifestyle. The Temple of Self preaches, "Never be content." While I understand the importance of pushing through challenges, there is an aspect of this statement that promotes anxiety and depression when people feel they can never be satisfied with who they are with all their human limitations. Could it be that our self-idolatry is the genesis of our bouts with anxiety and depression?

Jesus offers us a better way, a way to rest and peace through worshiping the one true God. He invites you, "Come unto me, all ye that labour and are heavy laden, and I will give you rest. Take my yoke upon you, and learn of me; for I am meek and lowly in heart: and ye shall find rest unto your souls" (Matt. 11:28-29).

The yoke of the Temple of Self is a heavy burden that leads to mental unrest because we feel like we've never done enough to measure up to this god's standards.

I hope by exposing this false god, you are no longer nose-blind to the characteristics of malignant narcissism. However, if we stop here, we do ourselves a great injustice. Paul did not end this chapter with "from such turn away." That is only step 1 of the five-part cure for this deadly recipe.

I promised we would move beyond the negative and end with a positive message of hope beyond the devastating effects of malignant narcissism. I am glad to tell you we are turning that corner now.

The Cure for Malignant Narcissism

If I held your nose too long under the stink of narcissism, let me apologize by offering the sweet, life-giving smell as given to us in the verses that follow the description of malignant narcissism in 2 Timothy 4.

Paul spelled out four more steps to cure malignant narcissism. How can we stop worshiping in the Temple of Self and turn to worshiping the one true God? This passage's fourfold positive strategy is to discover truth, follow godly examples, continue faithfully, and walk in God's Word. Let's unpack those concepts and discover how they will restore our souls.

Step 2 – Discover Truth

God will not stand idly by while idolatry floods our hearts, homes, and churches. One consistent theme throughout the Bible is that God always confronts the false gods and exposes them for the cheap imitations that they are. After He exposes the fakes, His goodness and greatness glimmer like the noonday sun.

Let's return to 1 Kings 18:20-46 to see how Almighty God exposed Baal on Mount Carmel. Baal was supposed to be in charge of the weather, among other powers. If any "god" could send lightning down from the sky, it should have been Baal.

Elijah stood with Almighty God against Baal's 450 prophets. They were so sincere in their prayers that they screamed at the top of their lungs and cut themselves for hours on end. The lightning never came. They sincerely believed in a lie.

Finally, Elijah said it was his turn. He built the altar and laid the sacrificial bull upon it, then he commanded it to be soaked in water. The water was poured all over the sacrifice and the wood until it filled a trench around the altar.

Elijah prayed a prayer that can be quoted in less than 30 seconds and the fire fell from heaven so fiercely that even the stones and the water in the trench were soaked up. He sincerely believed in the truth.

Almighty God left no question about who was the one true God. He exposed Baal as a fraud. The people standing by realized that the LORD alone is God. God brought the truth to light.

In 2 Timothy 3:9, Paul revealed what happens to the narcissistic false teachers who lead God's church astray, "But they shall proceed no further: for their folly shall be manifest unto all men, as theirs also was."

God knows how to expose those who oppose His truth and attempt to lead His children astray. Ultimately, they will stand before God as Judge one day to answer for their sin, but Paul spoke of the exposure of their lies in this lifetime, similar to how the false prophets of Baal were exposed by Elijah.

The Holy Spirit brings discernment into the minds of believers. I once heard this described as a "boloney meter." I remember speaking with a man who came to faith in Jesus when he was about 18 years old. He said growing up, the only knowledge he had of the name "Jesus" was as a curse word. He never went to church or heard the Gospel as a child. After a friend told him the truth about Jesus and how to be saved, he received Jesus as his Savior.

Some time later, he became homeless. A group of Christians helped him with necessities, so he started attending their church. The longer he attended, he had a nagging feeling that something just was off about the way they talked about God. His baloney meter was going off. It was really the Holy Spirit alerting him to false teaching.

This church was preaching a centuries-old heresy theologians call modalism. Simply stated, this view denies the Trinity and teaches that God is one in person. Like a single actor who plays three roles by going backstage to change clothes between scenes, modalism teaches that sometimes God appears as the Father; other times, He appears as Jesus the Son; and other times, He appears as the Holy Spirit, but it is only one person.

I've often wondered how modalists could explain the baptism of Jesus. The Bible describes Jesus standing in the water while simultaneously hearing the Father speak from heaven and viewing the Holy Spirit descending upon Jesus in the form of a dove, but I digress.

Recall Jesus' invitation in Matthew 11:28-30 is to come to Him to find rest. The context of His invitation is an appeal for people to come away from error and walk in God's truth. It's one thing to recognize false teaching, like the ingredients of malignant narcissism we picked apart in the previous section. It's quite another to know where to go next. If you move from one error to another, you've not helped yourself at all.

Returning to my example, the Holy Spirit was alerting this man that he was sitting under false teaching. That's Step 1 – recognizing error. Now he has a choice. Does he continue to stay in error by remaining at that church? Does he walk away from the church altogether? Does he find a church that teaches the Bible more correctly? This shows you how crucial this second step is—discovering the truth.

Thankfully, this man chose wisely. He left the church that taught error and found another church that teaches the Bible more correctly. He discovered the truth and chose to walk in it. This is the enjoyable place where the rest that Jesus promises is found.

However, the Temple of Self is filled with theological errors which cause all sorts of catastrophes in our lives. Sadly, some people never quit listening to those who are spreading humanism's false gospel. Not only can we rest in what God will do to call us away from error, but we can also rest in the fact that He will judge false teachers for leading others astray.

Some smooth-talkers can take bits of truth and mix them with lies to make something appear so good when it is poison. The serpent used the same tactic with Adam and Eve in the Garden of Eden. He took a bit of truth and mixed it with a lot of lies. Since it appealed to Adam and Eve's fleshly desires, they swallowed the fruit. They did not realize how big a hook was wrapped inside that tantalizing bait. Their focus of worship shifted from the one true God to the Temple of Self. In so doing, they plunged the human race under the curse of sin.

God did not sit idly by and watch them destroy their lives. He came to them in their brokenness and offered them a ray of hope amid their newly discovered darkness. Thankfully, they chose to follow God out of the darkness into His truth. Although we still feel the sting of their consequences to this day, God offered them the promise of redemption through the Messiah, Jesus (Gen. 3:15).

The narcissistic mindset that permeates these perilous times does not have to define us. While it promises to deliver everything we ever wanted, we quickly realize it is fool's gold. When we walk away from the fool's gold, we can find genuineness in walking with the one true God in His light and glorious freedom.

God invites us to speak His truth in love (Eph. 4:15). God's truth is the greatest treasure on Earth. We cannot afford to let it be hidden by lies. That leads us to the next fact.

Step 3 –Follow Godly Examples

Discovering truth creates within us a hunger to follow other godly examples who are walking in the truth. In contrast to the malignant narcissists, Paul reminded Timothy that he tried to set a positive example.

In 2 Timothy 3:10, Paul described his close relationship with Timothy by using the verb "fully known." This verb means to "watch closely" and to "follow." Timothy did not rely on what Paul told him about his life; rather, Paul lived this life out in front of Timothy and called him to remember this godly example.

Paul then listed characteristics that his life revealed in contrast with the negative narcissistic ingredients listed in 2 Timothy 3:2-5.

These characteristics included Paul's:

☐ *Doctrine – what he believed and taught about God*

☐ *Manner of life – how he lived out his belief in God*

☐ *Purpose – his whole-hearted devotion to God*

☐ *Faith – his whole-minded trust in God*

☐ *Long-suffering – his patience with people*

☐ *Charity – his unwavering love for God and others*

☐ *Patience – his endurance and steadfastness through trials*

☐ *Persecutions and afflictions – his suffering for the cause of Christ*

Paul reminded Timothy of the specific suffering he endured and then promised him, "Yea, and all that will live godly in Christ Jesus shall suffer persecution" (see 2 Tim. 3:12). That is a promise from God's Word that few want to claim. How many Christians are standing on that promise from God?

Paul did not sugarcoat it for Timothy. Following the truth will cost. However, Paul knew the long-term blessings of following the truth far exceeded the short-term costs. Elsewhere he put it this way, "For our light affliction, which is but for a moment, worketh for us a far more exceeding and eternal weight of glory" (2 Cor. 4:17). Paul had counted the cost of following the truth and he knew it was worth it. What a great example for Timothy, and us, to follow!

Step 4 – Continue Faithfully

Paul followed the promise of persecution with another not-so-positive promise. "But evil men and seducers shall wax worse and worse, deceiving, and being deceived" (2 Tim. 3:13). At first glance, this seems disheartening. Who wants to sign up for persecution and increasing opposition? How uplifting and encouraging is this message?

As we watch the rise of the one-world mind in our day, some Christians quote this verse as a vivid description of what we see happening in our world. I am not arguing they are wrong in their observation. However, if we fail to read the next verse, we rob ourselves of the understanding Paul wanted to impart to Timothy and the focus that we should have during these perilous times.

"But continue thou in the things which thou hast learned and hast been assured of, knowing of whom thou hast learned them" (2 Tim. 3:14). We have an important job to do in these perilous times. This is not the time to shrink back into the shadows. This is not the time to withdraw from the world.

When you are standing on the truth, there is no room for retreat. Paul did not have an ounce of quit in him and he urged Timothy to continue faithfully until the Lord called him home.

The temptation to quit will increase as the days grow spiritually darker. Resist that temptation. You will be tempted to remain silent in the face of opposition. Speak the truth in love with holy boldness. The malignant narcissists will take your truth-speaking as a personal attack. Do not compromise the truth but speak it with respect. Some people will be upset with you no matter how respectful you are. Be more concerned about pleasing God than you are about pleasing people.

We find a powerful example of this in Daniel's life. If you grew up in Sunday school, you are familiar with Daniel and the den of lions from Daniel 6. We will return to this powerful passage in Chapter 9 to uncover some more beautiful truths.

Daniel was singled out for continuing faithfully in his walk with God. He counted the cost and knew it was worth it to stand on the truth than to compromise his faith in God, even if it meant being cast into the den of lions. He had the respect of the king yet ironically, the king who made this law was powerless to change it. Only God could deliver Daniel.

"Persecutions" and "afflictions" are apt descriptions of the cruel death that surely awaited Daniel. Paul's next words fit in Daniel's life as well, "out of them all the Lord delivered me" (2 Tim. 3:11b). God shut the mouths of those hungry lions. When Daniel continued faithfully, he was delivered miraculously and God was glorified publicly.

What great things might God do in our day when we continue to faithfully stand upon what we know is truth? The malignant narcissists of Daniel's day were destroyed by the very trap they set for Daniel. God can thwart the schemes of humanity. Therefore, we should not live in fear of what they may threaten us with. Stand strong and continue faithfully!

It's one thing to stand strong in the face of adversity. It's another to know where our feet should stand. Paul told Timothy exactly where his feet of faith must be anchored. "And that from a child thou hast known the holy scriptures, which are able to make thee wise unto salvation through faith which is in Christ Jesus" (2 Tim. 3:15).

The Scriptures are our anchor. They are a firm foundation of bedrock truth that we can build our lives upon and trust our eternity in. In Step 5, Paul gave one of the most central passages on the authority of Scripture in the entire Bible as he explained this further to Timothy.

Step 5 – Stand on God's Word

As we arrive at the end of this powerful chapter, we reach two of the best-known verses from this book of the Bible, and perhaps from the entire New Testament.

"All scripture is given by inspiration of God, and is profitable for doctrine, for reproof, for correction, for instruction in righteousness: That the man of God may be perfect [complete, whole], thoroughly furnished [well-equipped] unto all good works" (2 Tim. 3:16-17).

These two verses are so straightforward, it is hard to misunderstand their message. Yet, could it be that we fail to appreciate the fuller context in which they are given? When we read these two verses, we might understand *that* Scripture is inspired by God, but the context of this chapter explains *why* God gave it to us for the perilous times of the last days.

God knew we would need His complete revelation to stand strong in the increasingly evil days. The word translated as "inspiration" in verse 16 means

Rise of the One-World Mind

"God-breathed." The 66 books of the Bible are the God-breathed words that we anchor our faith upon.

This verse goes on to explain the four-fold function of Scripture. Just like a GPS guides us on our journey from beginning to end, so, too, the Bible guides our faith through unfamiliar territory until we reach our destination and our faith is made sight.

First, God gave us Scripture for doctrine. When we follow our GPS down the road, we need to pay close attention to what it says so that we do not miss a turn. So, too ,Scripture reveals the truth we need to stand upon so that we can know God more deeply.

Sometimes, we misunderstand what the GPS says or we fail to pay attention to it and we make a wrong turn. What does the GPS start doing? It notifies us that we made a wrong turn. That is the second point Paul mentions —reproof. When we step out of God's boundaries, a proper understanding of His Word notifies us that we are wrong.

I am glad that the GPS doesn't leave us in error. It recalculates to bring us to our destination. That leads to Paul's third item in this list — correction. God did not give us His Word so He could constantly tell us how wrong we are. The bad news of our sin leads to the good news of the Gospel! God offers us a lifeline of hope to bring us out of the error of our sins.

Lastly, God's Word provides "instruction in righteousness." When we have returned to the right route, the GPS guides us to our destination turn by turn. So, too, God's Word is a lamp unto our feet, and a light unto our path, guiding our every step as we walk in His light (Psalm 119:105).

I see a summary and encapsulation of this entire chapter in these two verses. To cure malignant narcissism we must:

☐ *Recognize error – "reproof"*

☐ *Discover truth – "correction"*

☐ *Follow godly examples – "doctrine" and "instruction in righteousness"*

☐ *Continue faithfully – (verse 17)*

☐ *Stand on God's Word – (verse 17)*

If you have fallen prey to malignant narcissism, I encourage you to walk through these life-giving steps. Involve prayer in every step by first asking God to bring to your mind the errors you have bought into. Ask Him to reveal any malignant narcissism that may be lurking in your life.

Ask Him to help you discover His truth and to bring His truth to the surface in your life. Again, I reiterate the importance of God's Word. Your personal walk with God in Bible study and prayer will help you defeat malignant narcissism and will make you aware of what God is doing in our world today. You will be able to stand against narcissism and the rise of the one-world mind because you understand God's truth.

As you walk this journey, do not walk alone. Surround yourself with godly examples that you can follow closely. Ask God to bring these people into your life and give you the discernment to surround yourself with the right people.

As you take the next step, ask God to help you continue faithfully. Determine to stand strongly upon His truth amidst the perilous times we find ourselves in.

Lastly, remember that God has given us His Word to equip us with everything we need to excel right now. I know the spiritual battle is fierce. I know it is difficult to stand as a watchman in our generation. Yet, I also know that God has given us every spiritual resource we need to be spiritually strong for the times we live in. The difficulty of our days is no excuse for a lack of spiritual strength.

Amidst a selfish generation, God has provided a beacon of hope through His Word. May we boldly stand upon it and help others to find their way out of the Temple of Self and into the light of God's marvelous truth!

God's Word brings us comfort in knowing what will happen next and it gives us joy for the journey, no matter how bumpy the ride may get. As we enter the final chapters of this book, we will rely heavily upon God's Word to navigate us through the rise of the one-world mind.

LOOK UP!

Finally! You waded through the mire with me as we explored the rise of the one-world mind. We are navigating our way to the summit and ascending above the global turmoil brewing below. Now we get to turn our gaze on some beautiful truths as we learn how to live above the selfish, global mindset.

I used to take a group of teenagers to a Christian summer camp in the mountains of East Tennessee. One of the not-so-friendly competitions they offered was a mile and a half race up the side of a mountain.

Who thinks like this? "Hey, I've got a great idea! Let's meet at 6 a.m. and race up the side of a mountain!" Who would be crazy enough to sign up for that? A bunch of us. I admit, I signed up for it more than once over the years. There's something about being at church camp that makes you scream, "Yes, that's a great idea!" to some pretty ridiculous stuff. Plus, if you finished fast enough, they would give you a free T-shirt. Free clothes? I'm in!

As we gathered near the starting line, a bunch of sleepy-eyed teenagers and adults yawned and stretched as we prepared for the pain that surely awaited us.

The race started down in a valley, also known as a "holler" for us mountain folk. The first leg of the journey crisscrossed a creek in an ill-defined manner. Right out of the gate, our shoes and socks were soaked in pure Tennessee mountain spring water. That sounds heavenly. Doesn't it? I can tell you it is not. Wet socks and muddy shoes are not prime race conditions, especially when you're just getting started at the bottom of the mountain.

As we made our way past the stream, a few of us found some bees probably making pure Tennessee mountain honey in an old hollowed-out log. That sounds delicious. Doesn't it? I can tell you it is not. Did you know those bees sting when you try to jump over their log?

I've not even started my ascent up the side of the mountain and my shoes are soaking wet and my legs and ankles are itching with bee stings. The thought keeps going through my mind, "Why did I sign up for this? I could still be in bed."

Momma didn't raise a quitter, so I pushed on with all my might to reach the summit. As each racer arrived at the finish line on top of the mountain, we were greeted with cheers from the camp staff and picturesque vistas of mountains and lakes that stretched on for miles. The euphoria of accomplishing a challenging task with people you love turned temporary pain into a beautiful experience and wonderful memory.

High fives and smiles replaced winces. We made it! It didn't matter if you were the fastest or the slowest. All that mattered was that we all made it to the top together! The race is over. Now we can rest, bask in the early morning sunlight on the mountaintop, and enjoy some cold Tennessee mountain water, straight out of a multipack of plastic bottles from a supermarket. Plus, I got a free T-shirt! This beautiful day is just getting started.

I share this story with you because I believe it is a great example of what the church will experience. When we examine globalism, the Antichrist, and malignant narcissism, it feels like we are down in the valley. It's confusingly dark and the way out seems downright daunting. But a beautiful day is coming when we will be called up to be with Jesus forever. Until that day comes, we have God to guide us safely through this miry course one step at a time.

The darkness, the mud, and the stings will be forgotten as the beautiful eternal day begins! The Bible describes these powerful truths that give us a hopeful perspective during perilous times.

Consider these words, "O death, where is thy sting? O grave, where is thy victory? The sting of death is sin; and the strength of sin is the law. But thanks be to God, which giveth us the victory through our Lord Jesus Christ" (1 Cor. 15:55-57).

The next verse encourages us, "Therefore, my beloved brethren, be ye stedfast, unmoveable, always abounding in the work of the Lord, forasmuch as ye know that your labour is not in vain in the Lord" (1 Cor. 15:58).

If there is any verse that tells us how we should live in these perilous times, this is it. Join me for a brief Bible study to further understand how this verse teaches we ought to live today.

Paul, the author of 1 Corinthians under the inspiration of the Holy Spirit, tells us first to be "steadfast." A few generations before Paul's day, this Greek word was used to describe a rider who sat steady on the back of a horse. Isn't that a vivid picture of what it means to be "steadfast?"

Linked to this term, the following word is translated as "unmoveable" in the KJV. It means to not move away or shift. Similar to what we observed in 2 Timothy 3 in the last chapter, there is a temptation to move away from truth when perilous times come. On the authority of God's Word, I say, "Don't do it!" Be immovable as you stand on God's truth.

Interestingly, Paul encourages us to keep increasing in the work of the Lord. In an age of quitters, stand firm in your faith and increase your work in the Lord.

Notice I did not say, your work "for" the Lord. That is intentional. I've had seasons of life and ministry when I was busy "for" the Lord, but my service was rooted in people-pleasing. Suffice it to say, my people-pleasing work for the Lord led to burnout.[36] That is not what Paul is encouraging us to do.

Instead, we are reminded that the sacrifices of time, energy, and money we've given are never in vain. It may go unnoticed by others, but never by God. Hebrews 6:10 echoes this truth loud and clear, "For God is not unrighteous to forget your work and labour of love, which ye have showed toward his name, in that ye have ministered to the saints, and do minister."

Take heart and look up, my brothers and sisters in Christ. God's righteousness guarantees He will not forget your labor in His name. This is not the time to quit. Stand firm. Do not shift. Keep increasing your spiritual service in the Lord. Entrust the results into His hands since you know your labor is not in vain in the Lord.

Fear Not

Uncertain times are like simmering coals in a firepit. A crisis is like seasoned firewood thrown on the coals that awaken them into a blaze. A fire needs three ingredients to exist: fuel, oxygen, and heat. Without any one of these three, the fire will not burn.

If uncertain times are like heat and crises are like fuel, then fear is like oxygen. It blows across the embers and enables the fuel to burn hotter and faster. If you add more fuel to the fire, it will turn into an uncontrollable inferno. So too when crises overwhelm us, fear can create a destructive environment in a hurry.

---

36 I share much more about this in the second half of my book *Fake Jesus*. If this is something the Holy Spirit is speaking to your heart about, I would encourage you to check out the second half of the book and especially the chapter called "The 'Business Partner' Fake Jesus." Davis, Joshua R. *Fake Jesus* (Oklahoma City, OK: Beacon Street Press, 2023).

Why do you think God reminds us to not be afraid throughout the Bible? If you take oxygen out of the fire, guess what? It will smother out. If you handle your fear correctly, the heat and fuel will not burn within you. We cannot control or avoid uncertain times and crises. However, we can control our response to them. Fear is a response we can control.

When I was 15 years old, I couldn't wait to get my learner's permit to drive. However, when I began to drive on the road for the first time, I was afraid. The uncertainty haunted me. Learning to judge distance was challenging, especially when it came time to decide whether to slam on the brakes or the gas pedal when a light changed from green to yellow.

My dad also made sure I learned to drive a vehicle with a manual transmission. That brought in a whole other level of fear. Have you ever had to balance the gas and clutch pedals while stopped at a red light on a hill? That's not a fun skill to learn in traffic as a teenage driver.

It's been several years since then and I've driven many miles. My experience has removed the fear that once dominated my mind. I have moved from fearful to confident behind the wheel of a vehicle, even if it has a manual transmission and I'm stopped at a red light on a hill.

Uncertainty still exists on the roadways. The potential for crises is still present. My fear is not. My experience has taken the oxygen out of this potentially fiery situation.

Applying this analogy spiritually, the more we know God the easier it is to trust Him. If our God is too small, we become afraid that perhaps a particular crisis or time of uncertainty will be too much for Him to handle. Christians would rarely verbalize that they fear a circumstance is too much for Jesus to handle, but do our actions speak louder than our words when crises arise?

There is no situation that is too big for God to handle. No crisis catches Him by surprise. A man named Jairus came to Jesus with an emergency (Luke 8:40-56). His 12-year-old daughter was on her deathbed and he begged Jesus to come to his house. As Jesus hastened to Jairus' house, the crowd thronged Him.

If I were Jairus, I would have done anything possible to get the crowd out of the way so Jesus could get to my house on time to save my little daughter's life. This situation is on the verge of exploding into a blazing inferno.

The smoldering situation starts to smoke more and more when Jesus stops on his way to Jairus' house and asks the growing crowd, "Who touched me?" (Luke 8:45). Peter and the other disciples told Jesus to look at all the people around Him (Luke 8:45). How could they figure out who touched him? This fiery situation is escalating. Jesus recognized who it was and healed a woman who battled sickness for 12 years (Luke 8:45-48).

While Jesus spoke to the woman, a messenger came from Jairus' house with news that added fuel and oxygen to the smoldering uncertainty. The messenger said, "Thy daughter is dead; trouble not the Master" (Luke 8:49b). His message was that it was too late; nothing else could be done; leave Jesus alone. Jairus' inferno is about to blaze out of control.

Jesus heard the messenger and stepped in to take the oxygen of fear out of the equation. "Fear not: believe only, and she shall be made whole" (Luke 8:50). Jesus replied that it was not too late; something could be done; He was still in control. He called Jairus to trust that He was greater than this terrible crisis.

Jairus had a choice. Would he give into the oxygen of fear and explode in an inferno or would he trust Jesus to snuff out this fire? Thankfully, he trusted Jesus and allowed Him to remove the oxygen of fear from his fire.

When they reached Jairus' home, the fire was blazing as a crowd of mourners were beside themselves with grief. When Jesus attempted to remove the fearful oxygen from this fire by suggesting it was not too late, the crowd laughed and ridiculed Him instead of trusting Him (Luke 8:51-53).

To calm this inferno, Jesus asked for everyone to leave the house except for Peter, James, John, Jairus, and his wife. Jesus took the 12-year-old girl by the hand and simply said, "Maid, arise" (Luke 8:54b). With those words, the fire went completely out. The fuel of the crisis dissolved, the oxygen of fear evaporated, the heat of uncertainty cooled. The little girl arose immediately, alive and well! Mourning transformed into joy, fear transformed into faith, and God was glorified marvelously.

Jairus knew Jesus was greater than the uncertainty and the crisis his daughter faced. While others around Jairus called him to fear and doubt, he chose to trust the God who is greater. Jairus did not need to breathe the oxygen of fear.

Are Christians today breathing the oxygen of fear like the crowd around Jairus did thousands of years ago? Have we forgotten how great our God is? Have we failed to recognize that these uncertain times and the crises we face are in God's hands? Because of their doubt, the crowd missed seeing the miracle take place. What could we miss out on because we do not trust God?

Yes, perilous times are here. Evil is growing. We hear of wars and rumors of wars, earthquakes, famines, and deadly diseases. But we must remember that Jesus is greater than any force, power, or problem we will ever face. When fear of what might be threatens to overwhelm us, I think Jesus would speak the same words to you that He spoke to Jairus, "Fear not: believe only, and she shall be made whole" (Luke 8:50b).

In this book, I have warned you about the growing threats of globalism. I said from the outset that I did not want to leave you in fear. The reason we do not have to be afraid is the same reason Jairus did not have to be afraid – our God is greater!

When we face fearful circumstances, we need to press pause and remind ourselves that God is greater. Jairus chose to trust Jesus, even when it did not make sense. Others around him called him to give up on Jesus but Jairus displayed confidence in God no matter how impossible the situation seemed.

What could happen in our day if we chose to be confident in God like Jairus? What if we let God remove the oxygen of fear from the uncertain times and crises we face?

Over and over, God tells us not to be afraid. Consider these powerful words:

☐ *"Be strong and of a good courage, fear not, nor be afraid of them: for the LORD thy God, he it is that doth go with thee; he will not fail thee, nor forsake thee" (Deut. 31:6).*

☐ *"Have not I commanded thee? Be strong and of a good courage; be not afraid, neither be thou dismayed: for the LORD thy God is with thee whithersoever thou goest" (Josh. 1:9).*

☐ *"The LORD is my light and my salvation; whom shall I fear? the LORD is the strength of my life; of whom shall I be afraid?" (Ps. 27:1).*

☐ *"What time I am afraid, I will trust in thee." (Ps. 56:3)*

☐ *"He shall not be afraid of evil tidings: his heart is fixed, trusting in the LORD" (Ps. 112:7).*

☐ *"Fear thou not; for I am with thee: be not dismayed; for I am thy God: I will strengthen thee; yea, I will help thee; yea, I will uphold thee with the right hand of my righteousness" (Isa. 41:10).*

☐ *"For I the LORD thy God will hold thy right hand, saying unto thee, Fear not; I will help thee" (Isa. 41:13).*

☐ *"Peace I leave with you, my peace I give unto you: not as the world giveth, give I unto you. Let not your heart be troubled, neither let it be afraid" (John 14:27).*

☐ *"For God hath not given us the spirit of fear; but of power, and of love, and of a sound mind" (2 Tim. 1:7).*

I could go on and on for pages with similar verses. God does not want us to breathe the oxygen of fear. He wants us to rest in Him with a confident faith that knows He is always in control no matter how hot the uncertain times get or how much fuel a crisis brings our way.

Yes, the rise of the one-world mind is happening. Evil actions fill our newsfeeds. Personal crises occur without warning. We can choose to respond with fear or with faith in God. With Almighty God on our side, why should we be afraid of anything? Look up!

Sadly, one issue people express fear over is the rapture. A new term was created to describe this fear —rapture anxiety. What is it? How do we deal with it? Why is it rooted in misunderstanding the Gospel?

"Rapture Anxiety"

"Rapture anxiety" describes the fear or panic over the possibility of missing the rapture. I first wrote about this in the Prophecy in the News magazine's November 2022 issue.[37] God did not tell us about the rapture to scare us. The opposite is true. After Paul describes the rapture, he closes with the encouragement, "comfort one another with these words" (1 Thess. 4:18).

Further, a clear understanding of the rapture should bring us peace as we are, "Looking for that blessed hope, and the glorious appearing of the great God and our Saviour Jesus Christ" (Titus 2:13).

If the rapture produces anxiety, it is due to misunderstanding both the Word of God and the God of the Word. Thus, it becomes a Gospel issue. I will explain that more as we discuss the causes and cures of this anxiety, but first we must understand what it is.

The American Psychological Association in their Encyclopedia of Psychology defines anxiety as, "an emotion characterized by feelings of tension, worried thoughts, and physical changes like increased blood pressure." Couple that with a misunderstanding of the rapture, and a new phrase is created: rapture anxiety.

---

37 Davis, Josh. (2022, November). "Rapture Anxiety." *Prophecy in the News*, Nov. 2022, pages 8-10.

Some people began sharing their stories on their personal blogs and social media accounts. Several of those speaking out about their rapture anxiety now call themselves "exvangelicals," former evangelical Christians, who grew up afraid of the rapture.

Descriptions of personal experiences had similar traits. The typical story of rapture anxiety goes like this.

Imagine you are a young preteen or teenager who grew up believing in the Pretribulation rapture of the church.[38] You come inside the house after playing with friends outside and your good Christian parents are nowhere to be found. Anxiety sets in as fear floods your mind with thoughts like, "Did I miss the rapture? Where are my parents? Why didn't I go up in the rapture? Am I a wicked sinner that God does not love? Where should I go? Who can I call? Should I get the mark of the beast? How am I going to survive the Great Tribulation without my family or church?"

Forgive me for sounding like a medical commercial, "If you or a loved one have experienced these thoughts and feelings, you might have 'rapture anxiety.'" Here is free advice, no medical insurance needed: find the root cause and the cure for "rapture anxiety." Guess what? God's Word provides both.

Causes of Rapture Anxiety

The underlying causes of rapture anxiety are fear and doubt. These feelings are often accompanied by a works-based religious system and a misunderstanding of the Gospel message.

What you think becomes what you believe. What you believe forms your emotional responses. What you believe and feel becomes how you act. If I think wrongly about the Gospel, that will produce wrong beliefs and wrong feelings. This will produce wrong actions and responses, like rapture anxiety.

Let's walk through these causes to see how they can open the door to "rapture anxiety." Fear instantly sets in any time a young person cannot find his parent or guardian. That brief sense of fear is normal for any child. However, this fear can escalate to another level when the young person fears the absence of his parents means he has missed the rapture.

Fear of missing the rapture is often based on doubt. The young person doubts

---

38 If the term "Pretribulation rapture" is unfamiliar to the reader, please see the later section in this chapter which describes the Pretribulation rapture view.

whether he is truly saved from his sins. His mind swirls with spiritual doubts like, "Did I say the 'sinner's prayer' with the right words? What if I said it with the wrong attitude? What if I wasn't sincere enough when I prayed and asked Jesus to forgive my sins and save me? Did I say it with all my heart or did I say it because I wanted to please my parents or pastor?"

Underlying these doubts is another cause of rapture anxiety: a works-based religious system. The individual feels pressure to do the right things to ensure they check all the right religious boxes. For example, to check the "church boxes," they must show up for every church service, be involved in as many of the ministries of the church as possible, and serve the church leadership in any capacity asked of them.

Failure to check these boxes lands you squarely on God's bad side, and in the case of "rapture anxiety," could cause you to be left behind. Compound this with the guilt of sins committed, and you have a recipe for anxiety.

In a works-based religious system, the focus shifts from God to the individual. While claiming to be God-centered, the individual spends their energy appeasing their guilt. There is an inescapable religious to-do list. Living under this constant pressure to perform religious activities eventually produces burnout, stress, and you guessed it, anxiety. Coupling that with the weight of feeling unforgiven is enough to collapse anyone in despair. How much joy, peace, grace, and abundant life do you think would be inside a person who lives this way?

At its core, there is a deep misunderstanding of the Gospel of Jesus Christ in "rapture anxiety." The good news of freedom in Christ is turned into a works-based system of bondage. To a person living under this yoke of bondage, it matters little what Jesus has done for them when they compare that to all they must do for Him.

It would be discouraging and depressing to live under such a burdening system. No wonder people are running away from this kind of life. However, the answer is not abandoning the Christian faith altogether as some "exvangelicals" have done. Nor is the answer found in switching end-times views to a doctrine that denies the rapture. Later in this chapter, we will examine why the Pretribulation rapture view lines up best with Scripture. The right answer to this problem is to properly understand the Gospel of Jesus, which leads to a proper understanding of the rapture.

Cures for Rapture Anxiety

For every cause of rapture anxiety, there is a Bible cure. The essence of the answer we seek is found in a proper understanding of God's love. A me-centered, performance-driven, guilt-ridden, religious system is motivated by fear instead of love. The Bible says, "Fear hath torment." This is not the good news of Jesus.

Consider the verse where this phrase is found, "There is no fear in love; but perfect love casteth out fear: because fear hath torment. He that feareth is not made perfect in love" (1 John 4:18).

God has blessed me with a wonderful wife, and we have been happily married since 2009. We have a love-based relationship. But imagine what it would look like to have a marriage built on the causes of rapture anxiety, like fear.

Each morning, I would rush around, motivated by fear that I would not have enough hours in the day to do all I must do to please my wife. Is the coffee made correctly first thing in the morning? Check. Is breakfast to her liking? Check. Did I start the laundry? Check. Are the cars clean inside and out to please her? Check. Do we have enough money in the bank accounts to cover anything she might demand I buy her today? Check. Does she have everything she wants today? Check. The day is still young and I'm already exhausted.

If I lived like this day after day, month after month, year after year, I would experience guilt for not checking all the boxes all the time. I would doubt if she loved me, especially when I was tired or sick and unable to do all the checklist. I would be filled with constant fear, stress, and anxiety. How long do you think a marriage could last in that kind of scenario?

The Gospel of Jesus is a love-based relationship, not a performance-driven religious system. The focus of the Gospel is on what Jesus has done for us, not on what we do for Him, on who we are in Jesus, not on what we do for Jesus. The Bible is clear. A lifetime of good works is not enough to earn God's love, favor, grace, mercy, and forgiveness, yet He chooses to give it freely to all who would receive it (Eph. 2:1-10; Rom. 5:6-11, 10:13).

The anxiety over saying the sinner's prayer the right way with the right words disappears when we focus on Jesus. It's not about magic words. It's about simply receiving what He has done for us. When you receive a gift, do you have to say magic words before you can open it and enjoy it? No! There is no room for doubt when you base your faith on God's loving promises to you, such as those found in John 5:24 and 10:25-29. Receive and enjoy His gift to you today!

Jesus sets us free from checking the religious boxes. When you begin with the right relationship, the right works will begin to flow automatically. I don't do good works motivated by fear to earn my wife's love. When starting with love, it is a joy to serve her. It is a "want to," not a "have to." Thus, I am serving her with joy from acceptance not for acceptance. The same is true in my relationship with Jesus.

Christianity is the only religion in the world where God accepts us at the beginning of our relationship. With all other religious worldviews, one must wait till they die to find out whether their god accepted their works as good enough. Knowing you are accepted by God gives such peace, rest, and joy.

Correctly understanding the rapture brings tremendous comfort, not fearful anxiety. I began this section on rapture anxiety by quoting part of 1 Thessalonians 4:18, "comfort one another with these words." God did not reveal the rapture to scare us but to comfort us in uncertain times.

First John 4:17 tells us, "we may have boldness in the day of judgment." We can be confident in knowing where we are going when we die when we have accepted Jesus' invitation to follow Him.

Remember the comforting words Jesus spoke to give hope to His fearful followers, "Peace I leave with you, my peace I give unto you: not as the world giveth, give I unto you. Let not your heart be troubled, neither let it be afraid" (John 14:27).

Fear enters only when we misunderstand God's love as something we must earn. As we grasp God's unconditional love for us, "rapture anxiety" turns into "rapture anticipation."

Why should we believe in the rapture? How do we make sense of these Bible passages? Does the Bible tell us if the rapture will occur before, during, or after the Great Tribulation? How can this help us navigate the rise of the one-world mind?

Why I Believe in the Pretribulation Rapture of the Church

Before answering those important questions, we need to understand the terminology. Revelation 13 guided us through the rise of the one-world government, economy, and religion. As noted, those events will happen in the future Great Tribulation period.

Some critics like to point out that the word "rapture" is not in the Bible. They are correct. It is not. However, did you know the word "Bible" is not in the Bible? The word "Trinity" is not in the Bible either. I am not attempting to blow your mind or wreck your theology. The Bible is the inspired Word of God. It clearly teaches the doctrine of the Trinity, although it does not use that specific term. The same truth applies to the term "rapture." Just because the Bible does not use a specific term does not mean that doctrine is not taught in Scripture.

The word "rapture" is an English word based on the Latin word *rapiemur*, found in 1 Thessalonians 4:17 in the Latin translation of Scripture called the Vulgate. In the KJV, *rapiemur* is rendered "caught up." Both the Latin and English terms are translations of Greek, the original language of the New Testament.

Thus, the rapture is the "catching up" of the believers in Jesus Christ who are alive on earth when this moment occurs (1 Thess. 4:17). We will return to explain this event more fully. For now, let's continue with our terminology.

So far, we have the terms "tribulation" and "rapture." The last element of terminology deals with timing. When does the Bible say the rapture will occur? This gives rise to prefixes such as pretribulation, post-tribulation, or mid-tribulation rapture. These aren't the only views on the timing of the rapture, but they are representative of the majority views. Each of these views agrees that the rapture will take place but they disagree on when it will occur based on various interpretations of Scriptures.

The pretribulation view holds that the rapture will occur before the Tribulation begins. The mid-tribulation view holds that the rapture will occur at some point during the Tribulation. There are various interpretations within mid-tribulation viewpoints as to when exactly this will occur. The post-tribulation view holds that the rapture will occur at the end of the Great Tribulation. This means believers in Jesus will be raptured either before, during, or after the Great Tribulation.

Please note that brothers and sisters in Christ can disagree on the timing of the rapture and still be brothers and sisters in Christ. This end-times doctrine is important but it is not essential to salvation. As this chapter unfolds, I will make my case for holding the Pretribulation rapture view.

How Do We Understand Scripture?

Before launching into end-times theology, we need to take a step back and briefly discuss how to correctly understand what the Bible says. Should we understand the Bible literally? Are we free to interpret it non-literally?

For example, should we understand Jonah as a literal man who lived and who was swallowed by a whale? Or should we understand this as just a made-up story about a fictional character that conveys some sprinkling of moral truth?

History and archaeology have affirmed the Bible's accuracy over and over again. For example, many of the people, places, and obscure references Luke details in the book of Acts have been confirmed as totally accurate history.[39] Even liberal scholars admit that there is more historical evidence to support the crucifixion of Jesus than any other event from ancient history.[40]

How did Jesus view the Scriptures? Did He believe Jonah was real? How can this help us with the end times? What was Jesus' hermeneutic, His process of understanding the Scripture?

Jesus taught that the Old Testament Scriptures were to be taken literally. For example, in Matthew 12:39-42 Jesus affirmed that the prophet Jonah was swallowed by the whale and that the Queen of the South visited Solomon. In that one teaching, Jesus affirmed both Old Testament prophetic and narrative writings.

Jesus did not take the events of Jonah's and Solomon's lives as mythical literary inventions. He taught that they were historical figures and that those events described literally took place. This is not the only place in Scripture where Jesus does this. For instance, He affirmed Moses as the author of books of Scripture, a fact that some Bible skeptics deny (John 5:39-47).

Further, Jesus said in John 10:35, "The scripture cannot be broken." Jesus believed Scripture was infallible and inerrant. The Word was so central to Jesus that when Satan came to tempt Him three specific times, Jesus responded by saying, "It is written," every time (Matt. 4:1-11). Each quote Jesus gave back to Satan was straight out of Deuteronomy. Jesus not only knew the Word in His head, He hid the Word in His heart so that He could withstand Satan's strong temptation to sin (Psalm 119:11). In so doing, He was exemplifying

---

39 In my book, *Fake Jesus*, I explain some of these proofs in greater detail. See especially pages 63-78.
40 Ibid.

for us how we can overcome Satan and sin through the power of God's Word.

From these few examples, Jesus' hermeneutical principles begin to appear. He understood Scripture as the infallible, inerrant Word of God. He understood the characters and events of the Old Testament as literal and historical people, places, and events. Further, He applied Scripture to His daily life as He withstood Satan and walked closely with the Father.

Other New Testament Scriptures point to the inspiration and authority of Scripture in no uncertain terms. Perhaps the most well-known of these is 2 Timothy 3:16-17, "All scripture is given by inspiration of God, and is profitable for doctrine, for reproof, for correction, for instruction in righteousness: That the man of God may be perfect, thoroughly furnished unto all good works."

As noted in the preceding chapter, Paul used the word "inspiration," which means "God-breathed." God gave us the Bible to help us withstand Satan's temptations and walk closely in relationship with God.

Further, Peter referred to Paul's writings as "Scripture," even while the ink was still drying on Paul's epistles. Notice what Peter said in 2 Peter 3:15-16,

And account that the longsuffering of our Lord is salvation; even as our beloved brother Paul also according to the wisdom given unto him hath written unto you; As also in all his epistles, speaking in them of these things; in which are some things hard to be understood, which they that are unlearned and unstable wrest [twist], as they do also the other scriptures, unto their own destruction.

Peter affirms that Paul's writings are under the authority of God and that they should be considered Scripture.

To bring all this together, based on the authority of our Lord Jesus Christ and the clear teachings of His Word, believers should understand the Old and New Testament Scriptures as authoritative revelation from God. The Bible is the inspired, inerrant, infallible Word of God. Believers should understand biblical people, places, and events as literal and historical people, places, and events. But if we stop there and do not apply the Scripture to our daily lives, we are missing the reason God gave His Word in the first place. To borrow the words of D.L. Moody, "The Bible was not given for our information but for our transformation."

As we move forward in these uncertain times, we have God's certain truth to firmly plant our feet upon.

The order of this discussion is very important. The Bible forms our doctrine. Never get that cart before the horse. One cannot begin with their doctrine and force Scripture to fit into their preconceived mold. Anyone who does that is guilty of what Peter said in 2 Peter 3:16, twisting Scripture out of context. Bad interpretation breeds bad doctrine. Bad doctrine breeds false teaching and wrong behavior.

For example, suppose someone believes there is no resurrection of the dead. When they read about Jesus rising from the dead and promising His followers that He will also resurrect them, they are forced into a dilemma: they must either change their doctrine to fit what Scripture clearly says or distort Scripture out of context to fit what they already believe.

If they want to maintain their anti-resurrection doctrine, they will be forced to interpret biblical passages on resurrection as non-literal. If they do so, they will continue in their false teaching. Worse yet, they will continue living and believing there is no resurrection from the dead.

Paul wrote to combat this false belief in 1 Corinthians 15. He draws the implications of such a false belief and reveals how correct interpretation breeds correct doctrine. Then he masterfully showed how that proper doctrine inspires a confident and expectant hope in the future resurrection.

A proper understanding of God's Word is crucial to navigating these uncertain times. How does this understanding impact our view of the end times?

What Does Scripture Say About the Rapture?

When considering Scriptures that describe future events, we must understand what they say in a literal, historical, and grammatical manner. For example, the Bible's central passage on the rapture of the church is 1 Thessalonians 4:13-18. Take a close look at what this passage says and how it says it.

To start, 1 Thessalonians 4:14 says, "For if we believe that Jesus died and rose again, even so them also which sleep in Jesus will God bring with him." Notice how Paul demonstrated that correct interpretation leads to correct doctrine, which leads to correct behavior when he begins, "For if we believe that Jesus died and rose again."

The promise that follows inspires the same confident hope as 1 Corinthians 15. Notice this passage is written to and about believers in Jesus Christ. It specifically points out that God will bring those believers who have died "with him."

With Him where? The passage continues, "For this we say unto you by the word of the Lord, that we which are alive and remain unto the coming of the Lord shall not prevent [precede] them which are asleep" (1 Thess. 4:15). Paul made it clear that there will be some alive at the coming of the Lord.

The next verse continues, "For the Lord himself shall descend from heaven with a shout, with the voice of the archangel, and with the trump of God: and the dead in Christ shall rise first" (1 Thess. 4:16). Paul taught that those who have died believing in Jesus Christ will rise first. This is not a general resurrection of all people. This is a specific resurrection of only the "dead in Christ."

What will happen after that? The next verse reveals, "Then we which are alive and remain shall be caught up together with them in the clouds, to meet the Lord in the air: and so shall we ever be with the Lord" (1 Thess. 4:17). This verse plainly states that after God resurrects the "dead in Christ," those who are alive will "be caught up together with them in the clouds." Remember, the term "rapture" is derived from the phrase "caught up" in this verse.

Proper biblical interpretation demands we point out that this meeting is not on Earth; it is in the clouds. But wait, there's more. The next phrase confirms the purpose and place of this meeting: "to meet the Lord in the air." This meeting is not on Earth but in the air. How long will this meeting last? In a word, forever! As this verse says, "And so shall we ever be with the Lord."

Many other Scriptures discuss end-time events. As we correctly interpret each passage, we can compare Scripture with Scripture to help us build proper doctrine. When we do this, we realize some very important prophetic truths.

For example, 1 Corinthians 15:52 says "In a moment, in the twinkling of an eye, at the last trump: for the trumpet shall sound, and the dead shall be raised incorruptible, and we shall be changed." This speaks to the suddenness of the believers' resurrection as described in 1 Thessalonians 4:13-18.

This "suddenness" is often referred to as "imminence," meaning this resurrection and meeting in the air could take place at any moment without any prior warning or signs. However, the Scriptures that describe the Second Coming of Jesus to this earth reveal multiple signs and warnings that will occur beforehand.

This raises the question, are the rapture and the Second Coming the same event or separate events? Remember, Scripture must form our doctrine. Not the other way around. What does the Bible say about these events to help us correctly answer this important question?

While we cannot dive deep into every single Scripture on the rapture and the Second Coming, we can observe some significant differences between these two events. Dr. Norman Geisler compiled a helpful comparison chart that reveals the significant biblical differences between these two events.[41]

Rapture	Second Coming
Meeting them in the air (1 Thess. 4:17)	Taking them to the Earth (Zech. 14:4; Acts 1:11)
Taking believers to heaven (John 14:3)	Bringing believers back to Earth (Rev. 19:14)
Coming for His saints (2 Thess. 2:1)	Coming with His Saints (Jude 14)
Only believers see Him (1 Thess. 4:17)	All people see Him (Rev. 1:7)
No signs precede it (1 Thess. 5:1-3)	Many signs precede it (Matt. 24:3-30)
The Tribulation begins (2 Thess. 1:6-9)	The Millennium begins (Rev. 20:1-7)

Dr. Noah Hutchings also points out some crucial differences between the rapture and the Second Coming of Christ to Earth.[42] In the rapture passages, there is no mention of Armageddon, but the Second Coming to Earth occurs with the Battle of Armageddon. In the rapture, Jesus comes to save the righteous but in the Second Coming to Earth, He destroys the armies of the Antichrist.

Further, the book of Revelation reveals the rapture. Revelation 1-3 describes seven messages from Jesus to His seven churches. Included in Jesus' message to the sixth church is this promise, "Because thou hast kept the word of my patience, I also will keep thee from the hour of temptation, which shall come upon all the world, to try them that dwell upon the earth" (Rev. 3:10).

Some have said that this promise was to a local people for a time long past. However, notice that Jesus specifically promises they will be kept from the hour, the time, of temptation that will impact the whole world. He further explains it will be a time of testing for those who dwell upon the Earth.

Interestingly, Revelation 4-5 shifts the scene to heaven, followed by a vivid description of the future Great Tribulation in Revelation 6-18. There is no mention of the church in these chapters.

---

41 Norman L. Geisler, *Systematic Theology,* Vol. 4, "The Church and Last Things" (Bloomington, MN: Bethany House, 2005), 623.

42 Noah Hutchings, *Revelation for Today* (Bethany, OK: Bible Belt Publishing, 2010), 47.

We see the church again in Revelation 19 at the Marriage Supper of the Lamb in heaven. This is followed by the Second Coming of Jesus with His saints to the Earth (Rev. 20). The church is not on Earth during the Great Tribulation. Therefore, the context causes us to interpret Revelation 3:10 as a description of the Pretribulation rapture.

These passages help us conclude that the rapture and the Second Coming of Jesus are two separate events. Based on other passages that describe the imminence of the rapture and the fact that no signs precede it, we conclude that the rapture must take place before the Great Tribulation begins. Thus, the Pretribulation view of the rapture best interprets the Scripture consistently.

As Dr. Norman Geisler points out, "Many future features point to a Pretribulation rapture, which best explains all the data in a consistent and comprehensive manner. Only a Pretribulational rapture fits the signless imminence conveyed in many New Testament passages, and no other model explains the clear difference between the two aspects of His return."[43]

I believe in the Pretribulation rapture of the church because I follow the literal interpretation of Scripture, as Jesus and his apostles did, which in turn forms my doctrine, which in turn forms my belief and lifestyle.

I am listening for the trumpet to sound. I am filled with confident hope and am excited to be with Jesus forever. I hope you will be there with me through faith in what Jesus Christ did for us through His death and resurrection to provide eternal life for all who will believe. I hope to see you there!

I invite you to come up out of the mud and rest with us on top of the mountain. Gaze at the beautiful scenery. Stand firm upon the solid rock who is Jesus Christ.

Look up! Look with anticipation for the rapture of the church. The upward call could come any day. No prophetic signs will precede it. Let's be watching and waiting. God has a work for us to do until He calls us home.

---

43 Geisler, *Systematic Theology*, 623.

WHAT DO WE DO?

What should we do until the rapture occurs? How can we be ready for the rapture? As we observe the rise of the one-world mind, is there anything we can do to make a difference in our world today that could impact eternity?

Yes! The first step is to prepare for eternity. By "prepare," I am not offering advice on how to store food or water for the next 50 years; rather, I am addressing spiritual readiness. After we are prepared for eternity, we need to awaken as watchmen. Three Bible heroes show us how to get in the game and take a stand for the Lord in our day.

Often the final minutes of a ball game are the most crucial. When the competition is fierce and the game is on the line, the players need to be at their best. Their focus must be dialed in completely; they cannot be goofing off or falling asleep.

If we are living in the "final minutes" on God's prophetic clock before the rapture, we must maintain our focus. The Bible admonishes us often to watch – be alert, be focused, stay ready.

God has not left us here so that we can sit on the sidelines and watch the world decline into hell. He has put His church here in this moment with a purpose and for a purpose. We are here for "such a time as this" (Est. 4:14). It is time to get in the game with everything we have and everything we are. We have the greatest news the world can ever hear! We must seize this opportunity to draw closer to God and shine His light into the darkness around us.

Prepare

Appearances can be deceiving. My wife and I pulled into a fast-food restaurant to enjoy a milkshake while out for a date night. When we received our order, both our cups looked identical. Styrofoam cups were capped with clear plastic dome lids. A hefty portion of whipped cream and a cherry on top filled the dome. We stuck our straws in and began to drink.

Something was amiss. I ordered a chocolate milkshake with Oreo cookies mixed in. I suddenly realized my milkshake had neither chocolate nor Oreo cookies in it. The beautiful cup, the whipped cream, and the cherry concealed the mess that was supposed to be my milkshake. If it had been plain vanilla, that would be bearable. Instead, it was some kind of grayish goop that stuck to my teeth. I had to throw it away.

This illustrates an important end-times Bible truth. When Jesus described the end times for His disciples, He told them a parable about ten virgins (Matt. 25). We might call them "bridesmaids" today.

Jesus began His teaching by saying,

Then shall the kingdom of heaven be likened unto ten virgins, which took their lamps, and went forth to meet the bridegroom. And five of them were wise, and five were foolish. They that were foolish took their lamps, and took no oil with them: But the wise took oil in their vessels with their lamps. While the bridegroom tarried, they all slumbered and slept (Matt. 25:1-5).

During Jewish weddings of Jesus' day, the groom would leave the bride's home to return to his father's house. While there, the groom would prepare a place for both he and his bride to dwell. He would return to get his bride and a procession would commence back to his father's house where the wedding banquet would be celebrated. Torches would light the way through the darkness as the wedding party proceeded to the groom's home.

This is highly analogous to how the Bible describes the end times. Jesus left heaven, the Father's house, to come to this earth and call a bride to Himself. Before Jesus' death, resurrection, and ascension back to the Father, Jesus promised his disciples, "And if I go and prepare a place for you, I will come again, and receive you unto myself; that where I am, there ye may be also" (John 14:3).

The book of Revelation describes the wedding banquet, commonly called "The Marriage Supper of the Lamb" (Rev. 19:7-10). Following this wedding celebration is the Second Coming of Jesus to Earth with His bride (Rev. 19:11-16). This further indicates that the rapture will occur before the marriage feast and the Second Coming.

"For the Lord himself shall descend from heaven with a shout, with the voice of the archangel, and with the trump of God: and the dead in Christ shall rise first: Then we which are alive and remain shall be caught up together with them in the clouds, to meet the Lord in the air: and so shall we ever be with the Lord" (1 Thess. 4:16-17).

The groom calls His bride to Himself. She will be with the groom for all eternity from this point onward!

Who will be welcomed into the wedding celebration? Returning to Jesus' parable in Matthew 25, Jesus distinguishes between the wise and foolish bridesmaids. The only difference between the wise and foolish was oil for their lamps. The foolish had lamps but brought no fuel for them. The wise brought their lamps and sufficient oil.

All the bridesmaids agreed that the groom did not come back as soon as he was expected, so they "slumbered and slept" (Matt. 25:5). Why does the Bible distinguish between these two words? The word translated "slumbered" carries the idea of growing drowsy and nodding off to sleep whereas the word translated "slept" means that they were fully asleep. There was a time when they were watching and waiting but they all fell asleep.

While they slept, an unexpected call awoke them suddenly, "And at midnight there was a cry made, Behold, the bridegroom cometh; go ye out to meet him" (Matt. 25:6).

They immediately jumped into action. "Then all those virgins arose, and trimmed their lamps" (Matt. 25:7) Suddenly, the 5 foolish bridesmaids were interested in oil. "And the foolish said unto the wise, Give us of your oil; for our lamps are gone out" (Matt. 25:8).

The 5 wise who had oil knew there was no time to waste and not enough oil to share. "But the wise answered, saying, Not so; lest there be not enough for us and you: but go ye rather to them that sell, and buy for yourselves" (Matt. 25:9).

Each person was responsible for their oil. It couldn't be shared. So, the foolish went to buy some but they missed the groom. "And while they went to buy, the bridegroom came; and they that were ready went in with him to the marriage: and the door was shut" (Matt. 25:10).

They used their oil to light their way to the wedding celebration. When they reached the place where it was being held, they knocked on the door. "Afterward came also the other virgins, saying, Lord, Lord, open to us. But he answered and said, Verily I say unto you, I know you not" (Matt. 25:11-12).

These bridesmaids had no relationship with the groom. They were left on the outside looking in.

Just as my milkshake looked identical to my wife's on the outside, what was inside the cup was certainly not a milkshake. Yet what is inside the cup is what makes it a "milkshake." What I had pretended to be a milkshake but was not.

So too the foolish bridesmaids looked the part. They were waiting with the wise bridesmaids. They were in the right place at the right time but they were missing the main ingredient – the thing that would make all the difference in the world.

The groom did not reject them because they did not have any oil. When they knocked on the door, he did not say, "Sorry, you weren't ready when I called the first time." No, he said, "I know you not."

Their lack of oil was merely a revelation of what was truly missing – a relationship with the groom. This is what locked them out of the wedding celebration.

What will lock anyone out of heaven? The lack of a saving relationship with Jesus. How can you get into heaven? Only through a saving relationship with Jesus.

The wise bridesmaids who made it into the wedding celebration had a relationship with the groom. They awoke and went with him when the call came. Truly that is the only difference between these two groups.

Why would Jesus tell His disciples this? Have you heard the old saying, "preaching to the choir?" If any scenario fits that description, this appears to be it. The 12 had to be scratching their heads when Jesus told them this parable. They had lived with him for over 3 years at this point. They were his closest and most trusted followers and were serving in full-time ministry. Why speak to them about being locked out of eternity with God?

Matthew 26:14-16 reveals why Jesus told this parable to the 12. Judas Iscariot was one of the 12 who heard Jesus' parable. He looked like a devoted disciple of Jesus. He was in "full-time Christian ministry" for over 3 years! He had a leadership role and was looked up to by other devoted followers of Jesus. He served on "mission trips" for Jesus. He preached sermons about Jesus. He helped the needy in the name of Jesus. Yet the end of this man was one of the greatest tragedies the world has ever seen.

On the outside, Judas Iscariot had it all together but he was missing the most important ingredient of all – just like the foolish bridesmaids and my fake milkshake.

Was it too late for Judas Iscariot to get right with Jesus after he denied Him? Had he crossed a bridge too far to ever be redeemed and welcomed into heaven? No. Understand what Scripture says.

Do you recall how another of the 12 denied Jesus during His crucifixion? Simon Peter fulfilled Jesus' prophecy with pinpoint precision. Three times Peter denied that he knew Jesus.

Luke 22:60-61 reveals that as soon as Peter had finished his final denial of Jesus the rooster crowed, just as Jesus foretold. "And the Lord turned, and looked upon Peter. And Peter remembered the word of the Lord" (Luke 22:61a).

Imagine how gut-wrenching that moment was for Peter. He was so headstrong and self-reliant that he could not imagine a scenario where he would deny Jesus, and yet he did. At that moment, the eyes of Peter and Jesus met. No words had to be spoken. Peter understood how epically he had let Jesus down. Luke wrote Peter's response to this event, "And Peter went out, and wept bitterly" (Luke 22:62).

Simon Peter denied Jesus before the crucifixion. Judas Iscariot betrayed Jesus before the crucifixion. Peter wept bitterly. Judas hung himself (Matt. 27:3-5).

What was the difference between these two? Judas was filled with remorse but Peter repented. Remorse eats at you but never finds a resolution. Repentance is resolving your remorse. Peter allowed his remorse to drive him to repentance while Judas allowed his remorse to drive him to suicide.

Jesus forgave, restored, and recommissioned Peter (John 21). Truly, Peter's greatest ministry came after his greatest failure. Sadly, Judas thought he had crossed a bridge too far to be forgiven. Thoughts like, "How could Jesus ever forgive me after what I've done to Him," must have filled his mind. How different would the end of the story be for Judas if he had allowed his remorse to propel him into repentance?

No one is too far gone to ever be redeemed. Do not buy that lie. Allow your remorse to propel you to repentance. Ask God to forgive you of your sins and trust Him by faith. If He forgave Peter, He will forgive you too.

Judas looked the part on the outside but he never had a saving relationship with Jesus. Tragically, he ended his life instead of turning to the one who loved him and who could transform him. Thus, he was like the 5 foolish bridesmaids.

Why am I sharing all this with you? As we witness the rise of the one-world mind we need to be ready for eternity. The most important thing you can do today is to be sure you know Jesus is your Savior.

Christianity is not a code of conduct or a list of rules we must follow. My fake milkshake looked the part but it was utterly lacking the essential ingredient that made it a milkshake. The same was true for the 5 foolish bridesmaids and Judas Iscariot. Please do not let it be true about you.

There is a simple yet extremely important question we must all answer, "If I died today, where would I spend eternity?" Is it possible to know you are going to heaven? Jesus' disciple John wrote, "These things have I written unto you that believe on the name of the Son of God; that ye may know that ye have eternal life, and that ye may believe on the name of the Son of God" (1 John 5:13). Yes! We can know that we will go to heaven when we die.

How do we get to heaven? The Apostle Paul wrote, "For by grace are ye saved through faith; and that not of yourselves: it is the gift of God: Not of works, lest any man should boast" (Eph. 2:8-9). Simply stated, we cannot make it to heaven on our merit, but that is when Jesus stepped in. That is why He died on the cross for our sins.

Eternal life is not merely having a home in heaven when we die. It is a relationship with Jesus that begins now and lasts forever. Remember, the 5 foolish virgins were left out because they did not have a relationship with the groom.

Jesus invites you to begin an eternal relationship with Him today. "For God so loved the world, that he gave his only begotten Son, that whosoever believeth in him should not perish, but have everlasting life" (John 3:16). "For the wages of sin is death; but the gift of God is eternal life through Jesus Christ our Lord" (Rom. 6:23).

How can you receive this gift? "That if thou shalt confess with thy mouth the Lord Jesus, and shalt believe in thine heart that God hath raised him from the dead, thou shalt be saved… For whosoever shall call upon the name of the Lord shall be saved" (Rom. 10:9, 13).

There are no magic words that you must say to receive this gift. In your own way, express your heart to God, or make this simple prayer your own: "Lord Jesus, I know that I am a sinner and I need Your forgiveness. I believe that You died for me and rose from the dead. I want to turn from my sins and receive your gift of eternal life. Thank you for saving me today, Jesus! In Your name, amen."

Prepare for eternity today. You do not have to be left out or left behind. Jesus has gone to prepare a place for you. I look forward to spending eternity together with you!

Awaken

Jesus ended his Matthew 25 parable with a warning, "Watch therefore, for ye know neither the day nor the hour wherein the Son of man cometh" (Matt. 25:13). To whom did Jesus aim these words?

If this was a multiple-choice test, would the answer be a. Judas Iscariot, b. the 11, or c. all the above? The correct answer is c. all the above.

Recall from this parable that all the wise and foolish bridesmaids fell asleep while they awaited the call to go meet the groom. The foolish should have prepared before the call came, but they fell asleep. The wise should have been watching and waiting, but they too fell asleep.

Both the wise and foolish could have dealt with the lack of oil and discussed the need for a relationship with the groom before the call came. However, both groups grew tired of waiting for the groom and as he seemed to delay his coming, they fell asleep. When the groom's call came, it was too late to make any changes or further preparations.

The previous section was an urgent appeal to those like the foolish bridesmaids or Judas Iscariot to repent from sin and turn to Jesus for salvation today. However, there is also an urgent appeal for the believers, like the wise bridesmaids, to awaken out of sleep.

The church, the bride of Christ, has a responsibility in this world. Many people alive today are not prepared for eternity. Have churches fallen asleep thinking, "Where is the promise of His coming?" Preachers have talked about the rapture and the rise of the one-world mind for decades. There can be a temptation for Christians to think, "Here we go again. Another sermon about Bible prophecy. I've heard this all my life."

The church dozes off to sleep while going through religious motions. The wise bridesmaids were dressed and equipped with everything they needed then they fell asleep. Some believers are satisfied that they have "a ticket to heaven" and have fallen asleep while the world perishes around them.

Should not the wise bridesmaids have been more concerned about the foolish? Surely, they should have noticed the foolish were not prepared to meet the groom. The wise had something the foolish did not. Did they not care enough about the foolish to alert them to their need while there was still time to do something about it?

As we observe the rise of the one-world mind, the church cannot and must not sit idly by asleep until the rapture. Yes, our world is being conditioned to fall asleep and to receive the antichrist's system. However, this does not absolve the church's responsibility to remain awake and alert the world to what is happening.

I pray, in some small way, that this book will serve the church and the world to this end. Even before I started writing this book, I began praying, "Lord, open people's eyes." I admitted to you from the outset that my eyes were mostly closed as I nodded off. Thankfully, the Lord woke me up before I started snoring. I pray if you are like me, that you will wake up too.

Have you ever experienced this while driving? It was a busy Saturday at the end of a busy week. I was a seminary student living near Charlotte, North Carolina. I had worked all day and returned to my apartment to change clothes, grab my stuff, and drive over 3 hours to home.

I was about 45 minutes from home, driving in the dark on the interstate when I began to nod off. As my eyes closed for a couple of seconds, my head began to drop. I popped back awake, only to experience this several times in a row. Finally, my chin hit my chest and I popped awake with a surge of adrenaline. I knew I needed to pull off the road before I killed myself or someone else. I stopped at a convenience store and got some strong coffee. Once the caffeine kicked in, I was awake and able to drive the rest of the way safely home.

I fear many Christians are living this kind of spiritual life. We are heading home to be with Jesus forever, but we are nodding off to sleep the closer we get to home. It is dangerous for us and others around us. "Lord, open our eyes!"

The Apostle Paul challenged the Roman believers, "And that, knowing the time, that now it is high time to awake out of sleep: for now is our salvation nearer than when we believed. The night is far spent, the day is at hand: let us therefore cast off the works of darkness, and let us put on the armour of light." (Rom. 13:11-12).

Peter warned the first-century church, "But the end of all things is at hand: be ye therefore sober, and watch unto prayer." He learned this lesson the hard way before the crucifixion. Jesus prayed with His disciples in the Garden of Gethsemane just before He was arrested. Jesus told Peter to watch and pray so that he would not enter temptation. Three times Jesus found Peter asleep (Matt. 26:36-46). How many times did Peter deny Jesus? Three. How many times did Jesus restore Peter after His resurrection? Three (John 21).

In the Garden, Jesus set an example of what it means to watch and pray. Jesus knew the greatest challenge of His life on earth was soon coming. He knew how urgent it was to watch and pray.

Peter failed the first time, but now as an older man, he understood how important it was for the church to stay awake. As we witness the rise of the one-world mind and the gathering storm, should not we be watching and praying as well?

Southwest Radio Ministries' daily audio program is called "Watchman on the Wall." God prophesied through Ezekiel that He would give Israel a watchman to look out for approaching enemies (Ezek. 33:1-9).

The watchman had a solemn responsibility before God. When he saw the enemy coming, he was instructed to blow the trumpet and warn the people (Ezek. 33:3). If the people ignored the watchman's trumpet, their doom was on their own heads.

However, if the watchman saw an approaching enemy but did not warn the people, God would hold the watchman guilty for the death of anyone who was killed by the enemy under his watch (Ezek. 33:6). How serious this responsibility is! It must not be taken lightly. I have observed an increase in the number of Christians who refer to themselves as "watchmen." Before we assume this responsibility, first consider what we are placing ourselves under.

Imagine the watchman sat on the city wall night after night with nothing but a few scurrying animals to watch. He nods off to sleep one night, and the next night, and the next night. No one knows the watchman is asleep since they're asleep too. They think if something happens, he will wake them up and let them know. They trust that he is awake and watching. However, the enemy attacks and kills the unsuspecting people because the watchman is asleep. The watchman woke up too late to blow his trumpet of warning. God promised that their blood would be upon the watchman's hands (Ezek. 33:6, 8).

God told Ezekiel that He had made him a watchman for Israel (Ezek. 33:7). Ezekiel had the responsibility to warn the people about God's judgment coming upon them because of their sins. If Ezekiel kept quiet, God would hold him guilty (Ezek. 33:8). What a serious responsibility it is to be a watchman!

Pastors who remain silent about sin are sleeping watchmen. God will hold them responsible for not warning the people about the dangers of sin. While there is pressure on pastors to remain silent in the face of evil, they must remember that God will not hold them guiltless for people's spiritual destruction.

Some faithful watchmen are warning the people yet their warnings are ignored. These watchmen have done their job in the eyes of God. The responsibility is on the head of those who ignore the message.

Now, this does not give the watchman-pastor a license to "shear the sheep" in every message. There is a difference between sounding a trumpet of warning and constantly berating God's flock. Pastors are under-shepherds, not overlords (1 Peter 5:1-4).

All pastors are watchmen but not all watchmen are pastors. Many faithful Christians share messages in various means through various platforms to warn their families and others in their spheres of influence. It is wonderful that they have taken up this responsibility; however, I urge each watchman to consider the Lord's warning if they fail to sound the trumpet.

The 5 wise bridesmaids failed to sound the trumpet. They fell asleep and disregarded their responsibility as watchmen. The blood of the 5 foolish who were left out is on the hands of the 5 wise who failed to sound a warning. What a sobering thought!

Get in the Game

Would-be watchmen face a strong temptation to sit on the sidelines in silence when they consider the responsibility of a watchman along with the potential rejection they could face from the opposition. God does not want us to sit on the sidelines. He wants us to courageously step up. How can I make such a definitive statement? Because it is found throughout God's Word.

Moses' struggle to get off the sidelines is legendary. The book of Exodus describes how God miraculously preserved Moses' life when he was just an infant. Providentially, Pharaoh's daughter rescued Moses from the water and brought her into the royal palace to live as her son while Moses' mother got to serve Pharaoh's daughter as his babysitter. Only God could accomplish something so miraculous and providential!

Moses received the best education the Egyptians could offer. They trained him to be a leader in their nation. If Moses were alive today, we would consider him an up-and-comer, part of the "top 40 under 40" rising stars. He had so much potential.

The New Testament offers tremendous insight into this period of Moses' life. Just before Stephen is stoned, he retraces the history of God's working through Israel. He said of Moses, "And Moses was learned in all the wisdom of the Egyptians, and was mighty in words and in deeds. And when he was full forty years old, it came into his heart to visit his brethren the children of Israel." (Acts 7:22-23).

At 40 years old, Moses had the skills and abilities to be a great leader. Acts 7:22 says he was "mighty in words and deeds." No doubt Moses sensed the pressure of leadership from an early age. His mother must have told him how God preserved his life for a special reason. Moses knew God put him in this special place to deliver his people out of Egyptian slavery.

As a 40-year-old man, Moses took matters into his own hands. He jumped in to stop an Egyptian from beating an Israelite slave. Moses killed the Egyptian man in the process. He must have thought this would ignite a movement among his people to escape Egypt under his leadership. This was his moment to shine!

Acts 7:25 provides a telling detail, "For he supposed his brethren would have understood how that God by his hand would deliver them: but they understood not." What was supposed to be Moses' moment to shine turned into a life-altering disaster. Moses fled from Egypt and tended sheep in the wilderness of Midian for 40 years.

The prime of his life felt wasted. Had his hard work, education, and leadership training been for naught? Even worse, had his miraculous deliverance at birth been a mistake? Self-doubt must have flooded Moses' mind during his prime of life from 40 to 80 years old. He went from the "top 40 under 40" to a nobody, seemingly a waste of tremendous potential.

Why do I say that? When God appeared to Moses in the burning bush, Moses was filled with excuses. He thought he was on the sideline for good. He blew his opportunity to lead and thought a second chance was just a pipe dream.

God had other plans. He called Moses to go to Pharaoh and led the Hebrews out of Egyptian bondage. Moses' story wasn't over. His failure wasn't final. God used Moses' preparation differently than Moses expected but we must remember that God's ways are higher than our ways.

Moses' miraculous deliverance at birth wasn't a lucky accident. It was a divine intervention. His training wasn't years of wasted effort; however, God knew what needed to change in Moses before he was ready to lead. God knows the same thing about us too.

God told Moses to go back to Egypt and even gave Moses two signs to verify that God had sent him to deliver them – his staff would turn into a snake and his hand became leprous then miraculously healed (Ex. 4:1-9). In case these two were not enough, God even gave Moses a third verification – water he poured on the ground from the Nile River would instantly turn into blood (Ex. 4:9).

If this were still not enough, God made it unequivocally clear to Moses that He would be with him every step of the way. God would guide and guard Moses as he led the people to the Promised Land. With God on our side, why should we fear anyone or anything?

Even with all this, Moses faltered. "And Moses said unto the LORD, O my Lord, I am not eloquent, neither heretofore, nor since thou hast spoken unto thy servant: but I am slow of speech, and of a slow tongue" (Ex. 4:10). At 40, Moses was a man mighty in words and deeds but at 80, he felt so weak and inadequate to lead.

God rejected Moses' excuses and called Moses to trust Him. "And the LORD said unto him, Who hath made man's mouth? or who maketh the dumb, or deaf, or the seeing, or the blind? have not I the LORD? Now therefore go, and I will be with thy mouth, and teach thee what thou shalt say" (Ex. 4:11-12).

With Almighty God promising to be with him every step of the way, surely Moses would obey. Yet he still refuses to trust God and follow by faith. "And he said, O my Lord, send, I pray thee, by the hand of him whom thou wilt send" (Ex. 4:13). Could this unusual turn of phrase be Moses' attempt to show God he couldn't speak eloquently? Is he trying to prove to God that he is not the man he was at 40 – mighty in words and deeds? What is Moses trying to communicate in this phrase? His statement means, "Lord, please send someone else." What a sad and faithless prayer to pray!

God became angry at Moses' lack of trust and obedience. "And the anger of the LORD was kindled against Moses, and he said, Is not Aaron the Levite thy brother? I know that he can speak well. And also, behold, he cometh forth to meet thee: and when he seeth thee, he will be glad in his heart" (Ex. 4:14).

Moses was reluctant to get off the sidelines and into the game. His reluctance was rooted in a lack of trust in God. Could it be that we are reluctant to get in the game because we do not trust God? We give excuses for why we cannot be watchmen even when we sense God is calling us to step up.

Moses felt like he couldn't do it. Guess what? He was right! He couldn't do it on his own, but he had God with him, leading and directing him every step of the way. On our own, we can accomplish nothing for the kingdom of God, but with God, we can conquer anything He calls us to.

Moses' biggest obstacle was neither Egypt nor getting his people to trust him. His biggest obstacle was his lack of faith in the one true God.

If anything will keep us on the sidelines, that is it. The smaller our view of God is, the smaller our faith and trust in God will be. The converse is also true. The bigger our view of God is, the greater our faith and trust in Him will be.

Although he was reluctant at first, Moses eventually got off the sidelines and into the game. What we remember the most about Moses came from the last third of his life, from age 80-120.

As age increases, people feel like their usefulness to God decreases. Their prime is past. They can't do what they used to do. This cannot be an excuse to sit on the sidelines and watch others play the game.

As long as we are on this Earth, God still has a game plan for us. The game plan will change as we age, but that is not an excuse to sit on the sidelines. What spiritual victories could be accomplished if we simply trust and obey Almighty God?

This is not just an admonition for older adults to get back in the game. It is an admonition for people of all ages to stand courageously and trust God completely.

One of the most famous sections from the Apostle Paul's epistles is the "armor of God" passage in Ephesians 6. Immediately after he described the armor we must have for the spiritual battle, he encouraged people to pray. "Praying always with all prayer and supplication in the Spirit, and watching thereunto with all perseverance and supplication for all saints" (Eph. 6:18).

Prayer is a spiritual weapon no watchman can be without. Do you see how he linked praying with watching? Spiritual alertness is a result of a deep prayer life. Notice Paul's personal prayer request in the next two verses.

"And for me, that utterance may be given unto me, that I may open my mouth boldly, to make known the mystery of the gospel, For which I am an ambassador in bonds: that therein I may speak boldly, as I ought to speak" (Eph. 6:19-20).

Paul knew that the spiritual battle would tempt him to get on the sideline and stay silent. He asked people to pray that he would have the boldness he needed to proclaim the Good News of Jesus as a faithful ambassador. This is a powerful prayer we need to pray today! May the Lord give us holy boldness to speak His truth in love.

Stand Strong in Battle

How can we make a difference as we watch the rise of the one-world mind? Sometimes a watchman can feel like a lonely place to be. A man once told me that people at his church looked at him like he had cauliflower growing out of his ears when he talked to them about the rise of the one-world government and economy.

There is a temptation to quit watching and warning when other Christians ignore or criticize our stand. We want to sit comfortably on the sidelines like other Christians. However, if we are truly called by God to be a watchman, we cannot sit on the sidelines for long. There will be a burning within our souls to proclaim God's truth.

Jeremiah was a watchman who spoke God's warnings of judgment to people who should have been on his side. After being publicly humiliated by ungodly priests at the house of the Lord, Jeremiah was tempted to keep quiet. However, it was a losing battle.

Jeremiah said, "I will not make mention of him [God], nor speak any more in his name. But his word was in mine heart as a burning fire shut up in my bones, and I was weary with forbearing, and I could not stay" (Jer. 20:9).

What a vivid description of a true watchman! The fire of God's message burned within him until he could not contain it any longer. He felt as if he would die if he held it in. He couldn't sit on the sidelines in silence, he had to get back in the game. He did not care what it cost him personally, he knew he had to speak God's truth.

Another popular Bible character acted almost opposite of Moses and revealed a powerful example of great faith in a great God. It is one of the most famous accounts in the Bible. Kids in Sunday school learn about this account from an early age – David and Goliath. This event is recorded for us in 1 Samuel 17.

There is a danger with "familiar" Bible stories. We learn the basic details and miss some of the rich spiritual truths they convey. Worse, we misapply them to our lives. The account of David and Goliath was not given in God's Word to help us overcome our giants; rather, it shows us how great God is and how we can walk with Him by faith.

Consider some of the lessons we can learn from this episode of David's life to help us stand strong on God's side in this present battle against the rise of the one-world mind.

First, we must learn to ignore the critics. Both Jeremiah and David faced criticism from people who should have stood strongly with them and encouraged them to follow the Lord's leading. Sadly, the church is not immune to this today.

David's father sent him with some supplies to aid Israel's army as it faced the Philistines and their gigantic champion – Goliath of Gath. He would face criticism from the outset.

If we back up slightly in this narrative, we understand that Saul is the first king of Israel. They wanted a king like the other nations even though Almighty God was supposed to be their King. This grieved the heart of the Prophet Samuel. "But the thing displeased Samuel, when they said, Give us a king to judge us. And Samuel prayed unto the LORD" (1 Sam. 8:6).

God's response to Samuel reveals the true heart of the people. "And the LORD said unto Samuel, Hearken unto the voice of the people in all that they say unto thee: for they have not rejected thee, but they have rejected me, that I should not reign over them" (1 Sam. 8:7).

They rejected God's authority over them before they rejected God's messenger, Samuel. This is a powerful truth spiritual leaders must understand. Christian leaders will face rejection from people when they stand for God's truth properly but the Christian leader must remember the people rejected God's authority before they rejected the leader.

Saul became king and led Israel's army into battle against the Philistines, as we return to 1 Samuel 17. When Israel's warriors saw the size of Goliath and heard his taunts, they were scared to death. "When Saul and all Israel heard those words of the Philistine, they were dismayed, and greatly afraid" (1 Samuel 17:11).

When God's authority is rejected, the results are abysmal. Israel should have trusted in the Lord their God to defeat the enemy. However, their small view of God caused both them and their hand-picked king to be crippled with fear in the face of the enemy.

Along came a fresh-faced shepherd boy who had a big view of God. As David arrived in Israel's camp, his oldest brother Eliab criticized David's presence and misjudged David's motives (1 Sam. 17:28). Eliab's lack of discernment proved that he was far away from God.

David was faced with his first of many crossroads in this episode. Would he listen to his eldest brother's criticism and his attempts to shame David into going back home to the little flock of sheep? David responded to Eliab, "What have I now done? Is there not a cause?" (1 Sam. 17:29). Then David turned to talk to other people. In other words, David chose to ignore the critical voice of his brother and honor God above all others.

Criticism from family often stings more than criticism from other sources. Like David, we must consider the source of the criticism. If it is rooted in truth, we ought to consider correcting our decisions, but if, like Eliab, it is rooted in the wrong spirit, we need to ignore it and go forward with what God wants us to do.

As we face the rise of the one-world mind in our generation, there will be criticism from others, perhaps even our own family. If they truly love the Lord, we should consider what they have to say if perhaps we have become imbalanced in how we are presenting God's truth. However, they might try to discourage us so that they can protect their own ego or unbiblical priorities. How can we tell the difference? Consider the contrast between constructive criticism and destructive criticism.

Constructive criticism seeks to build you up while destructive criticism seeks to tear you down. Constructive criticism has your best interests at heart while destructive criticism wants to hurt, embarrass, or shame you. Constructive criticism offers correction in a way that will help you. Destructive criticism seeks to defeat and discourage you. Constructive criticism reveals the individual cares about you while destructive criticism reveals they do not.

David's second challenge came from King Saul. David could not rush in against Goliath without obtaining King Saul's permission first. When David sought permission to fight Goliath, King Saul said, "Thou art not able to go against this Philistine to fight with him: for thou art but a youth, and he a man of war from his youth" (1 Sam. 17:33). While King Saul is not critical of David, he gave David a reality check.

David is faced with a second crossroad in this episode. Should he acquiesce to the king's authority or should he go forward with what God wants him to do? Goliath was much larger than David. King Saul wasn't wrong. However, even the king was not close to the heart of God. Saul was looking as people look, on the outward appearance, but David was not looking at Goliath. He was looking at God.

As David made his appeal to King Saul, he told how God had delivered him from a lion and a bear while he was watching his flock of sheep. David made it clear, "The LORD that delivered me out of the paw of the lion, and out of the paw of the bear, he will deliver me out of the hand of this Philistine" (1 Sam. 17:37). David did not base his ability to fight Goliath on his strengths but on the authority of Almighty God.

This separated David from all the others. It will separate us from the crowd of naysayers, skeptics, and doubters too.

King Saul gave David his blessing but then tried to put him in his royal armor. David decided to take that armor off and picked up five smooth stones for his sling instead.

This teaches us that God has a unique path for each of us to follow after Him. Your path is not my path. My path is not your path. Other faithful watchmen are writing books and producing valuable content. Each one is unique in their presentation and emphases. I should not try to be like another Christian leader because God has made me as He wants me to be. He has placed me where I am for His greatest glory and my greatest good.

David faced a third crossroad when he came face to face with the giant Goliath. Goliath did his best to intimidate, embarrass, and mentally defeat David's spirit before the fight began. He promised to destroy David that day. Would David run in fear before fighting the giant? Would he listen to the threats, insults, and intimidation?

Professional athletes know that the mental preparation is as important as the physical preparation. If an athlete thinks they cannot compete, they set themselves up for failure. If they allow the taunts of their opponent to get in their head, this distraction will rob their concentration from playing the game.

As we watch the rise of the one-world mind, this battle is invisible. No literal giant is standing before us in glistening armor, attempting to throw a massive spear through us. However, the mental and spiritual battle is very real. If Christians allow themselves to be defeated by the enemy in their minds, they will stay on the sidelines and not engage in the battle as watchmen on the wall.

How did David respond to Goliath's insults and intimidation tactics? With one of the most faith-filled statements in this book of the Bible.

> Then said David to the Philistine, Thou comest to me with a sword, and with a spear, and with a shield: but I come to thee in the name of the LORD of hosts, the God of the armies of Israel, whom thou hast defied. This day will the LORD deliver thee into mine hand; and I will smite thee, and take thine head from thee; and I will give the carcases of the host of the Philistines this day unto the fowls of the air, and to the wild beasts of the earth; that all the earth may know that there is a God in Israel. And all this assembly shall know that the LORD saveth not with sword and spear: for the battle is the LORD's and he will give you into our hands (1 Sam. 17:45-47).

Did David say he was going to defeat Goliath with a sling and a stone? No! David did not enter this battle in his own strength. Instead, he relied on the one true God of all heaven and Earth to deliver Goliath into his hands. Yes, the battle belonged to the Lord and God proved that He alone is the one in control!

Goliath had controlled the narrative for 40 straight days until one unlikely man stepped forward with confidence, not in himself, but in his great God. Goliath spewed a message of fear and dread to scare Israel into staying on the sidelines.

Today, powerful people attempt to control the narrative. The liberal news media is in lockstep with the one-world agenda of our day. As I pointed out early on in this book, fear is weaponized to brainwash people into getting in line with the one-world mindset.

We face a mighty Goliath today. On our own, we are no match for this Goliath but with God, this Goliath is no match for us! After David spoke these words to Goliath, he took action. He did not run in fear nor did he stoop to Goliath's level to fight a merely human battle. David constantly relied on God and faced the giant in God's strength.

This showdown reaches its climax when David and Goliath charge toward one another. The Bible says, "And David put his hand in his bag, and took thence a stone, and slang it, and smote the Philistine in his forehead, that the stone sunk into his forehead; and he fell upon his face to the earth" (1 Sam. 17:49).

David defeated the giant! Sports broadcasters still use the analogy of David vs. Goliath when a heavy underdog is facing an opponent who seems superior in every way. Truly, Goliath was superior to David in every aspect except one – who they worshiped – but that was the most crucial aspect of all.

As Christians, we are not fighting for victory. Jesus won the victory through his death and resurrection. We fight from victory. The Apostle Paul encouraged the Roman Christians, "Nay, in all these things we are more than conquerors through him that loved us" (Rom. 8:37).

The Goliath of globalism is no match for God. Bible prophecy makes it clear that the one-world government, economy, and worship will be a short-lived empire. At the end of the 7-year Great Tribulation, Jesus will return to Earth and the Antichrist and False Prophet will be cast into the Lake of Fire (Rev. 19:20-21).

At the end of the 1,000-year Millennial Reign of Jesus on Earth, Satan will be cast into the Lake of Fire as all evil is quarantined forever (Rev. 20:10-15). The new heaven and Earth will emerge as God's followers enjoy eternity together with Him!

Why should Christians be discouraged or intimidated in the battles we face today? "The LORD is on my side; I will not fear: what can man do unto me?" (Psalm 118:6).

Stand Firm in Faith

The pioneer Baptist Missionary to China, Hudson Taylor (1832-1905), wrote a letter to a fellow missionary who sought to take the Gospel into a difficult area of China. Taylor's China Inland Mission team attempted to enter this area for about 10 years with no success. He offered sage advice to the missionaries going to this difficult province, "you must go forward on your knees."

Truly, the army of Christ is the only army that advances on our knees. As noted previously, the Apostle Paul understood how potent prayer is in the spiritual battle the church faces (Eph. 6:18-20).

Another beloved account of a Bible hero provides a powerful paradigm for us as we witness the rise of the one-world mind. In a culture intent on brainwashing people into conformity, Daniel stood out from the crowd. Let's return to learn some more lessons from the life of this faithful follower of God.

Just as David stood alone against the enemy, Daniel stood alone against the evil attempts to obliterate his influence. Were they alone when they took their stand? Certainly not! With the Lord on our side, even one person can be a majority.

Never count out Almighty God. He alone can transform the impossible into the possible. Hudson Taylor is credited with saying, "I have found that there are three stages in every great work of God. First, it is impossible, then it is difficult, then it is done." How true!

Daniel faced multiple brainwashing attempts throughout his life. In Chapter 1, I discussed how the Babylonians attempted to transform Daniel as a teenager. Now in his 80s, Daniel witnessed the Medes and Persians conquer the Babylonians and attempt to unite the various factions of their new world order. I think they attempted to sell this to the public as a way to establish unity in the new kingdom. How did they attempt to do this? More about that momentarily, but the Scripture reveals their real motivation upfront in the beloved passage commonly called, "Daniel and the Den of Lions."

Daniel 6 reveals the real motivation of this new world order was jealousy. The Medes and Persians had 120 princes, also called satraps, who answered to 3 overseers, also called presidents or administrators. These 3 overseers answered only to the king. Daniel was appointed as one of the 3 overseers and as the king observed his wisdom and skill, he promoted him over the other 2 overseers and all 120 princes, thus Daniel became second only to the king in this new world order (Dan. 6:1-3).

How do you think these rulers felt after spending years working up through the political ranks as they elbowed each other out of the way? It was finally their time to shine on the world stage. Their plans to dominate the Babylonians worked perfectly. Through their skillful fighting and maneuvering, Babylon was conquered. They are ready to enjoy the fruits of their labors and extend their power throughout their vast empire.

Imagine how angry they must have been when the king appointed a Jewish holdover from the Babylonian captivity as one of three overseers in the new world order. Why should a captive rule over them? How demeaning it must have felt for these Persian rulers to be forced to serve under Daniel.

They hatched their manipulative plan which was sold to the king as an attempt to unite their empire's different factions. They told the king, "All the presidents of the kingdom, the governors, and the princes, the counsellors, and the captains, have consulted together to establish a royal statute, and to make a firm decree, that whosoever shall ask a petition of any God or man for thirty days, save of thee, O king, he shall be cast into the den of lions" (Dan. 6:7).

Lying and manipulative politicians are nothing new. Had "all" the presidents (overseers) agreed to this plan? They made it seem like Daniel was in total agreement with this scheme when he was the target of their conniving plans. So, the king, thinking all were in agreement, signed the decree into law.

Daniel had a choice to make once he heard that this new law passed without his knowledge. First, he could have started a revolt against the new world order by uniting the Babylonians and other captives. He could have rushed to the "media" to expose the manipulative plans and raised an army to rebel against the princes who wanted to control every aspect of their lives, including who they could worship.

Under this option, Daniel would have fought anger with anger and human power with human power. Daniel did not choose this option. He did not stoop to their level.

Secondly, Daniel could have remained silent. He could have passively gone along with the decree without saying anything. It was just for 30 days. He could have worshipped God in private for 30 days and not made a big deal out of this decree. After all, the king had placed him as second-in-command. Why ruin such a prestigious position by publicly disobeying the king's royal decree? Why stand as an obstacle to the unity of the new world order? Daniel did not choose this option either.

Instead, Daniel chose option 3, "Now when Daniel knew that the writing was signed, he went into his house; and his windows being open in his chamber toward Jerusalem, he kneeled upon his knees three times a day, and prayed, and gave thanks before his God, as he did aforetime" (Dan. 6:10).

Instead of fighting anger with anger and human power with human power, Daniel advanced his fight on his knees. Like David, he fought human power with God's strength instead of his own. He stood his ground and publicly demonstrated his commitment to the one true God above all other allegiances.

Daniel cared more about offending God than any other human being, even the king whom he served. He knew this was a life-and-death decision, yet he chose to follow God and pray as he always had.

God did not deliver Daniel from facing the den of lions. Sometimes we think that when we take a stand for God and for what is right, He will deliver us from the fight. He might deliver us *from* the fight but other times he delivers us *through* the fight. Both Daniel and David courageously trusted God as they stared death in the eye. Both were delivered through the valley of the shadow of death by the one true God who is greater than any force or scheme.

I once heard a preacher say that Daniel did not face a "lion's den." This English possessive case makes it appear that the lions owned the den. No, the Bible says it was a "den of lions." The lions did not own the den, God did!

As Daniel was cast into the den of lions, King Darius pointed to Daniel's God as the Divine Deliverer, "Thy God whom thou servest continually, he will deliver thee" (Dan. 6:16c).

Although the king could not deliver Daniel from his foolish decree, the king recognized that the power of Daniel's God was far superior to his own. In pride, the king signed the decree to exert his authority over his new world order but now in humility, he is forced to admit there are powers far greater than his own.

King Darius could not sleep a wink that night and as soon as the sun came up, he ran to the den of lions. The Bible says, "And when he came to the den, he cried with a lamentable voice unto Daniel: and the king spake and said to Daniel, O Daniel, servant of the living God, is thy God, whom thou servest continually, able to deliver thee from the lions?" (Dan. 6:20).

This king was the leader of the new world order and was the most powerful man in the world. Yet, once again we witness his weakness on display. His power was limited, his knowledge was limited, his wisdom was limited, his foresight was limited, his legal authority was limited, and his kingdom, as vast as it was, was limited. A man with so many resources at his fingertips was unable to deliver his most trusted advisor from certain death.

Adding to his list of shortcomings, the Bible says King Darius spoke with a "lamentable voice." The word translated as "lamentable" carries the idea of grief, sadness, distress, and pain. His sleepless night was spent in fear and regret because he did not have much confidence that Daniel would survive. His understanding of Daniel's God was severely limited yet he had enough faith to ask if Daniel was, by the slimmest of chances, still alive.

Daniel's testimony of faith in his God was enough to convince the king at this point that perhaps Daniel's God is the one true God. If you are wondering what it means to "let your light so shine before men, that they may see your good works, and glorify your Father which is in heaven," this is it (Matt. 5:14). Daniel's prayer pointed to his close relationship with, dependence upon, and total commitment to Almighty God.

Imagine the king's delight when he heard a strong voice answer him. "Then said Daniel unto the king, O king, live for ever. My God hath sent his angel, and hath shut the lions' mouths, that they have not hurt me: forasmuch as before him innocency was found in me; and also before thee, O king, have I done no hurt" (Dan. 6:21-22).

The king's belief in Daniel's God skyrocketed immediately. His mood changed from sadness to joy in less than 30 seconds. The next verse says, "Then was the king exceeding glad for him, and commanded that they should take Daniel up out of the den. So Daniel was taken up out of the den, and no manner of hurt was found upon him, because he believed in his God" (Dan. 6:23).

"Because he believed in his God." These powerful words summarize the secret strength of Daniel. He advanced on his knees through faith in a great God. I did not say great faith in God, but faith in a great God.

Our belief is only as good as the object we put it in. Imagine I walked into a room with two chairs. One is broken and rickety and the other is strong and sturdy. Which one should I sit in? The strong and sturdy one, of course. I place my belief in the strong chair and my sitting in it displays my trust in it. If our view of God is too small, our trust in Him will be too. However, once we realize how great He is, we can trust Him with everything.

As the account continues, King Darius called for the enemies of Daniel who hatched this diabolical plot to be cast into the den of their own making. They were instantly destroyed by the hungry lions (Dan. 6:24). What a stunning reversal!

This prompted King Darius to set the public record straight and dispel the fake news that was spread about Daniel.

Then king Darius wrote unto all people, nations, and languages, that dwell in all the earth; Peace be multiplied unto you. I make a decree, That in every dominion of my kingdom men tremble and fear before the God of Daniel: for he is the living God, and stedfast for ever, and his kingdom that which shall not be destroyed, and his dominion shall be even unto the end. He delivereth and rescueth, and he worketh signs and wonders in heaven and in earth, who hath delivered Daniel from the power of the lions (Dan. 6:25-27).

The king was initially impressed with Daniel's wisdom and skill but after Daniel survived the den of lions without so much as a cat scratch, the king was more impressed with Daniel's God. His new decree extolled Daniel's God more than it did Daniel. This watchman lit the way for the king to see God more clearly. Daniel's life constantly pointed others to the one true God.

When Daniel chose to fight in God's strength instead of man's, he was delivered God's way, his enemies were put down God's way, and the record was set straight in God's way. Plus, God was glorified throughout the whole earth through this one man's faith. What is for God's greatest glory is also for our greatest good.

As we seek to stand against the rise of the one-world mind, we do well to heed Daniel and David's examples. Both David and Daniel stood in the power of God against an enemy that should have easily defeated them.

Both David and Daniel witnessed a stunning reversal as God defeated and destroyed their enemies. The ones who thought they had the upper hand were cast down by the one true God.

Both David and Daniel stood alone. There is no mention of help from any source other than God, but once again I say that one with God is a majority.

Years ago, conservative Christians in America touted the "Moral Majority." Without making a political comment, I simply ask, was this an attempt to fight anger with anger, numbers with numbers, and human strength with human strength?

Is the American church continuing to decline because we stand in human strength instead of God's strength? I once heard a wise and seasoned pastor ask this question to a group of pastors, "How much of what the church does

Rise of the One-World Mind

each week could continue even if God did not exist?" What a probing question!

Both Daniel and David cared more about glorifying God than their popularity, platform, or legacy. In other words, both cared more about the name of God than their names. Both were used by God to mightily advance His kingdom on this Earth. Whose name do you care more about – yours or God's? "Yours" can mean simply yourself, but it can also apply to your church, your ministry, your school, your group, or your family.

Daniel and David offer us a paradigm for standing strong with God against the rise of new world powers who oppose God and His truth. This is the kind of watchman the world needs to see today. I ask, will you be this kind of watchman on the wall? Will you stand in God's strength, even if that means standing alone?

REMEMBER!

People tend to remember what they should forget and to forget what they should remember. Consider a humorous example of this truism from the life of the revered scientist, Albert Einstein.

One day after Einstein had moved to his home at the Institute for Advanced Study in Princeton, N.J., the telephone rang in the office of the Dean of the Princeton Graduate School. The voice at the other end inquired: "May I speak with Dean Eisenhart, please?" Advised that my father was not in, the voice continued: "Perhaps then you will tell me where Dr. Einstein lives." My father's secretary replied that she could not do this, since Dr. Einstein wished to have his privacy respected. The voice on the telephone dropped to a near whisper: "Please do not tell anybody, but I am Dr. Einstein. I am on my way home, and have forgotten where my house is!"[44]

It is laughable to think that a man so admired and respected in the scientific community for his brilliant mind would forget something as basic as where his house is. However, some admired and respected Christians have forgotten the same truth – they have forgotten this world is not their home.

Constantly staring at the rise of the one-world mind will cause us to forget where our home is. That is why we need to discuss where our focus must be as we close this book.

The brainwashing world is trying its best to cause us to forget. We must determine that we will remember the Lord and His truth. The Babylonians wanted Daniel and his friends to forget their homeland, forget their faith, and forget their God. Daniel "purposed in his heart" to remember his homeland, his faith, and his God (Dan. 1:8). He stood out from the crowd and God used him to change his world because he remembered the most important truths in all the world.

Remember Eternity

Followers of Jesus live in the unique tension between the "now" and the "not yet," between the temporal and the eternal. The Bible is filled with admonitions

---

44 Paul Lee Tan, *Encyclopedia of 7700 Illustrations: Signs of the Times* (Garland, TX: Bible Communications, Inc., 1996), 455.

to live for eternity instead of the here and now.

Jesus' beloved "Sermon on the Mount," found in Matthew 5-7, calls us to remember eternity. Jesus revealed that people can give, pray, and fast for the glory of people instead of the glory of God (Matt. 6:1-18). He pointedly said they received their reward when people took notice, but God did not take notice. Even their act of "worship" was living for the temporal instead of the eternal.

Jesus summarized this by saying, "Lay not up for yourselves treasures upon earth, where moth and rust doth corrupt, and where thieves break through and steal: But lay up for yourselves treasures in heaven, where neither moth nor rust doth corrupt, and where thieves do not break through nor steal. For where your treasure is, there will your heart be also." (Matt. 6:19-21).

What does it mean to live for eternity? It means to remember that the stuff of this world will one day be no more. When God ushers in the new heaven and earth, all the "stuff" of this world will be gone. Yes, God blesses us in the here and now, but if our focus is only on this moment, we are missing so much that God has for us.

I have a tote of trophies and recognition awards from my school days. When my wife and I moved to a new house in 2012, they went straight into the attic. When we moved again in 2021, I opened the tote for about 30 seconds just to see what was in it, then they went straight into the basement. My nostalgia tells me to keep them. My wife tells me to get rid of them, but as long as they are in a corner of the basement, they're forgotten by us both.

These awards are gathering dust and rust. I never bump into an old friend who asks, "Do you remember the school awards night from 6th grade? Man, you accomplished something great that year!" I don't know if I won anything in 6th grade. I don't remember who won academic or athletic awards from 6th grade. The funny thing is, I struggle to remember what any of those awards are without finding and opening that tote.

Those are all earthly treasures that will fade away. They are not eternal. Yes, it is good to recognize people for their hard work and accomplishments. I have nothing against that at all. However, how often do we honor people who achieve temporary victories yet fail to honor those who lay up treasure in heaven?

Quick, without looking, can you tell me who won the Super Bowl, World Series, and NBA championship in 2004? I like sports, but I cannot tell you that. I would struggle to tell you who won those three championships last year. Temporary victories come and go. Athletes who win championships are eventually forgotten. We try to keep their accomplishments alive by talking about how great they were, but eventually, their memory fades as the generations who saw them compete pass away.

This is not meant to discourage you nor to discourage athletic pursuits; rather, it is simply to show how temporary these victories are. The encouraging news is that we can invest in eternity and truly make a difference in this world that will last far beyond us.

How can we invest in eternity? People have eternal souls and all of us will spend eternity in either heaven or hell. Therefore, investing in people is investing in eternity. Developing a close relationship with God is investing in eternity. Focusing on God's good news amid a bad news world is investing in eternity. The church is eternal, so strengthening your brothers and sisters in Christ is investing in eternity.

The Bible is filled with admonitions to live for eternity. Truly, an entire book could be written about this subject. Consider these powerful verses.

"After these things the word of the LORD came unto Abram in a vision, saying, Fear not, Abram: I am thy shield, and thy exceeding great reward" (Gen. 15:1). God called Abram to keep his focus on eternity, not on the here and now. God's promises to Abram would impact eternity, so God called Abram to remember the eternal priorities above the temporary.

"For since the beginning of the world men have not heard, nor perceived by the ear, neither hath the eye seen, O God, beside thee, what he hath prepared for him that waiteth for him" (Isa. 64:4). The entirety of Isaiah 64 encourages us to use our time in the here and now to prepare for eternity. God has a wonderful eternity in store for those who love Him, but judgment awaits those who reject Him.

Paul wrote, "But as it is written, Eye hath not seen, nor ear heard, neither have entered into the heart of man, the things which God hath prepared for them that love him. But God hath revealed them unto us by his Spirit: for the Spirit searcheth all things, yea, the deep things of God." (1 Cor. 2:9-10). Some consider verse 9 as a reference to heaven. While that certainly applies, heaven is not specifically mentioned in this passage. Instead, it speaks about the deep wisdom found in God's eternal Word. God has great blessings for both now and eternity through His Word.

Peter referred to Isaiah 40:7-8 when he wrote, "For all flesh is as grass, and all the glory of man as the flower of grass. The grass withereth, and the flower thereof falleth away: But the word of the Lord endureth for ever. And this is the word which by the gospel is preached unto you" (1 Peter 1:24-25).

Even if we live to age 100, what is that in comparison with eternity? It is less than a drop of water in the Atlantic Ocean. We are blessed with a brief window of opportunity to receive and promote the Good News of Jesus. God's Word is eternal, so taking eternity seriously must involve taking God's Word seriously.

In fact, 1 Peter is peppered with eternal reminders. Peter wrote to Christians who faced discouraging trials. Keeping an eternal perspective helps us navigate difficult trials with our eyes fixed on Jesus.

"That the trial of your faith, being much more precious than of gold that perisheth, though it be tried with fire, might be found unto praise and honour and glory at the appearing of Jesus Christ: Whom having not seen, ye love; in whom, though now ye see him not, yet believing, ye rejoice with joy unspeakable and full of glory" (1 Peter 1:7-8).

"But the God of all grace, who hath called us unto his eternal glory by Christ Jesus, after that ye have suffered a while, make you perfect, stablish, strengthen, settle you" (1 Peter 5:10).

Peter knew what it meant to suffer the pain of rejection, antagonism, and physical harm for the cause of Jesus Christ. Yet he willingly endured it all because he kept his eyes on eternity.

Paul had the same perspective. "For which cause we faint not; but though our outward man perish, yet the inward man is renewed day by day. For our light affliction, which is but for a moment, worketh for us a far more exceeding and eternal weight of glory" (2 Cor. 4:16-17).

Let's press pause before we consider the next verse. Paul encouraged the Corinthians to not give up in the face of persecution. He considered all the severe difficulties he faced as light and momentary afflictions because he understood the eternal good that resulted from it, both for himself and others.

This passage continues, "While we look not at the things which are seen, but at the things which are not seen: for the things which are seen are temporal; but the things which are not seen are eternal" (2 Cor. 4:18).

If there is one verse that summarizes all that I have attempted to communicate to you in this section, that is it. Watching the rise of the one-world mind is ultimately temporary. If watchmen warn about the rise of the one-world mind but never point people to eternity, we have missed the whole point of being a watchman.

Some popular personalities warn of the approaching storm but only admonish people to buy gold, protect their families, and store supplies. They do not mention eternal preparation. Thus, they are unqualified to be biblical watchmen.

I am not advocating for a lack of preparation. We certainly should do all we can to protect our families and our freedoms. However, when our focus becomes solely on the here and now, we have left our biblical responsibility to prioritize eternal preparation above temporal preparation.

A family could survive a "zombie apocalypse" yet still perish in their sins and spend eternity in hell. The greatest preparation one can make is to be ready for eternity. It is pointless to prepare to survive in this world if we are not ready for what comes after death.

As Christians, we must remember, "If ye then be risen with Christ, seek those things which are above, where Christ sitteth on the right hand of God. Set your affection on things above, not on things on the earth. For ye are dead, and your life is hid with Christ in God. When Christ, who is our life, shall appear, then shall ye also appear with him in glory" (Col. 3:1-4).

A Christian's most important citizenship is not which country they live in on this Earth because Christians are first and foremost citizens of eternity in heaven. Paul urged the Philippians to keep this in mind. "For our conversation is in heaven; from whence also we look for the Saviour, the Lord Jesus Christ" (Phil. 3:20). The rare Greek word translated as "conversation" carries the idea of citizenship and belonging to a commonwealth. This would have carried great weight with the original Philippian readers. Bible commentator Richard Melick explained this important historical background.

> *Immediately their thoughts would have turned to an analogy with their earthly citizenship. They were proud of their Roman citizenship, but the analogy would have conveyed more. Philippi was an outpost colony, and, interestingly, Paul was at the home base in Rome.*

Regularly they awaited news from the capital to know how to conduct their business. When Paul said that they belonged to a citizenship, he spoke directly to them. Though they belonged to a city, the political entity spanned several geographical areas. Similarly, the church was an outpost of an entity that had its own capital, heaven. Although "citizenship" may call to mind a place, Paul used it of a people. They awaited the Savior from that citizenship. He would come with power sufficient to subdue everything and with ability to transform their bodies to be like his. They would naturally associate subduing power with a Roman emperor, but transforming power was unique to Christ.[45]

Paul called them to remember where their citizenship was, but he also called them to look for the Savior, the Lord Jesus Christ. The word translated as "look" carries a sense of eagerness. One commentator said it "suggests a tiptoe anticipation and longing."[46]

Are you living with tiptoe anticipation for eternity with our wonderful Savior, Jesus Christ? Are you preparing now for eternity?

Remember Heaven

Jesus' 12 disciples were overwhelmed. More than 3 years of full-time Christian ministry seemed to unravel before their very eyes. As they ate what is now called the Last Supper, Jesus reminded them that his death was coming soon (John 13). As the evening continued, Satan entered into Judas Iscariot in a devilish attempt to conquer Jesus once and for all (John 13:21-30).

Discussing death brings feelings of sadness, loneliness, and finality. Jesus' followers longed to be with Him, but He prepared them for His death. "Simon Peter said unto him, Lord, whither goest thou? Jesus answered him, Whither I go, thou canst not follow me now; but thou shalt follow me afterwards" (John 13:36).

Imagine how John felt as he wrote those words and remembered the pain of those moments. How heartbreaking these moments must have been for John to relive through his writings. He next revealed Peter's reply, "Lord, why cannot I follow thee now? I will lay down my life for thy sake" (John 13:37).

If discussing death and facing Satan weren't enough, Jesus also predicted Peter's denial in His reply to Peter's question. "Jesus answered him, Wilt thou

---

45 Richard R. Melick, *Philippians, Colossians, Philemon*, vol. 32, *The New American Commentary* (Nashville: Broadman & Holman Publishers, 1991), 143–144.

46 Robert P. Lightner, "Philippians," in *The Bible Knowledge Commentary: An Exposition of the Scriptures*, ed. J. F. Walvoord and R. B. Zuck, vol. 2 (Wheaton, IL: Victor Books, 1985), 662.

Rise of the One-World Mind

lay down thy life for my sake? Verily, verily, I say unto thee, The cock shall not crow, till thou hast denied me thrice" (John 13:38).

You might be thinking, "I thought this section was about heaven. This is depressing!" It was in this moment that Jesus spoke words of comfort and hope that would cause His followers to remember eternity. Knowing He was facing His death, Jesus chose to speak about eternal life as He revealed the reality of heaven.

Jesus' very next words were, "Let not your heart be troubled: ye believe in God, believe also in me" (John 14:1). First, Jesus instructed them to not allow their emotions to cause them to forget the proper perspective. They could have easily been overwhelmed with grief and confusion to the point they would give up.

Jesus moved beyond what to avoid and instructed them on what to do – "Believe in God, believe also in me." Believe is a key word in this Gospel. As the cross approached, the disciples' faith would be tested like never before. They witnessed Jesus miraculously raise Lazarus from the dead, so they knew He was the Messiah, God in the flesh. Jesus called them to continue to trust Him even when it seemed impossible.

These words were spoken to Jesus' disciples but were not intended only for them. They are words spoken to all of Jesus' followers. The rise of the one-world mind can trouble us. Trying to figure out what will happen next will confuse and bewilder us. We fight the temptation against letting our hearts be troubled. We must take Jesus' words to heart – trust Him!

Jesus revealed that this temporary separation would not be the end of the story. "In my Father's house are many mansions: if it were not so, I would have told you. I go to prepare a place for you" (John 14:2).

At this point, there is a temptation to get hung up on the size and architecture of heaven. However, this misses the point of what Jesus expresses. If Jesus wanted His followers to have a blueprint of heaven, don't you think He could have given them one in this passage?

His point wasn't to describe some ethereal skyscraper or a land filled with castles and Victorian mansions; rather, Jesus wanted them to know that He was going to prepare a place for them in His Father's house. He is calling them to remember a person, not a place; a "who," not a "what."

Their impending separation would cause grief, heartache, loss, and loneliness. Jesus spoke words of comfort to their souls to remind them that He would not forget about them because He would be preparing a place for His followers to come be with Him forever.

Heaven is a very real place. Please do not confuse my refusal to debate the meaning of the word translated as "mansions" as a denial that heaven is an actual place. If it were not a real place, why would these words bring comfort to followers of Jesus?

Some get the idea that when Jesus said, "I go to prepare a place for you," He is busy in heaven building places for every follower until the rapture call comes. I can almost hear a preacher say, "The carpenter's Son is busy building you a home in the sky!" That's not what Jesus is saying. "The Gospel of John is not trying to portray Jesus as being in the construction business of building or renovating rooms. Rather, Jesus was in the business of leading people to God."[47]

Remember the historical context of this passage. When Jesus first spoke these words to His disciples, the cross and resurrection were still future. Jesus' earthly mission was not yet complete when He first spoke these words but through His death and resurrection, a way would be prepared for all who will believe to go to the Father's house forever!

Jesus continued, "And if I go and prepare a place for you, I will come again, and receive you unto myself; that where I am, there ye may be also" (John 14:3). The statement "I will come again" does not appear to be a reference to His resurrection but to the rapture when He will receive His followers unto Himself and take them to be with Him forever. Yes, He came again at the resurrection, but He later ascended away from them back into heaven.

Further, Jesus told His followers that they know both where He is going and the way to where He is going. "And whither I go ye know, and the way ye know" (John 14:4). Jesus had taught His disciples how to get to heaven through a relationship with God, yet Thomas asked, "Lord, we know not whither thou goest; and how can we know the way?" (John 14:5).

Thomas wanted Jesus to provide turn-by-turn directions like a GPS but to use a GPS, you have to know the destination. Remember, the cross and resurrection

47 Gerald L. Borchert, *John 12–21*, vol. 25B, *The New American Commentary* (Nashville: Broadman & Holman Publishers, 2002), 105.

were still in the future for Thomas and the rest. They had some pieces of the puzzle but they still could not put it all together, so Jesus made it clear to His followers with His famous reply.

"Jesus saith unto him, I am the way, the truth, and the life: no man cometh unto the Father, but by me" (John 14:6). It is impossible to make it to heaven on our own. No GPS in the world will give us directions there.

"Not by works of righteousness which we have done, but according to his mercy he saved us, by the washing of regeneration, and renewing of the Holy Ghost; Which he shed on us abundantly through Jesus Christ our Saviour; That being justified by his grace, we should be made heirs according to the hope of eternal life" (Titus 3:5-7).

Peter later proclaimed, "Neither is there salvation in any other: for there is none other name under heaven given among men, whereby we must be saved" (Acts 4:12). There is only one way to get to the Father's house – Jesus.

To make such a statement seems anathema to this postmodern age, but consider this. How could all these claims be equally true? Atheism says death is the end, there is no afterlife, no heaven. Hinduism says we will be reincarnated back into this world based on how moral we were in our previous life. Christianity says people are eternal and will spend eternity in either heaven or hell. These three are contradictory. Someone must be right and someone must be wrong.

Thus, Jesus' claim to be the way, the truth, and the life must be true or false. His words would only be words of comfort if He really is the way, the truth, and the life. After they encountered the resurrected Jesus, these worried disciples turned the world upside down as they boldly proclaimed that Jesus is the way, the truth, and the life![48]

Yes, heaven is a real place, and the only way to get there is through faith in Jesus. When the rise of the one-world mind threatens to unnerve us, we must remember this world is not our home. Because of Jesus, we have something wonderful to anticipate!

While much remains a mystery about heaven, the Bible reveals all we need

---

48 It is outside the scope of this book to provide a full apologetic for Jesus' deity at this juncture. However, my book *Fake Jesus* spells this out in great detail. There are other great works one could consult, such as Geisler, Norman and Frank Turek. *I Don't Have Enough Faith to Be an Atheist* (Wheaton, IL: Crossway, 2004).

to know about it on this side of eternity. Revelation 21-22 describe beautiful truths about the new heaven and new Earth that God will create after sin, Satan, and evil are forever quarantined in the lake of fire (Rev. 20).

John wrote, "And I saw a new heaven and a new earth: for the first heaven and the first earth were passed away; and there was no more sea. And I John saw the holy city, new Jerusalem, coming down from God out of heaven, prepared as a bride adorned for her husband (Rev. 21:1-2).

As noted in the discussion on John 14, the focus is not primarily on describing the structure of heaven, but on the One who is the focal point of it all — Almighty God. Notice John wrote that the new Jerusalem is "prepared as a bride adorned for her husband." The word "prepare" is the same Greek word used in John 14 when Jesus promised to go prepare a place. Promises made, promises kept!

John continued, "And I heard a great voice out of heaven saying, Behold, the tabernacle of God is with men, and he will dwell with them, and they shall be his people, and God himself shall be with them, and be their God" (Rev. 21:3).

Jesus promised to bring His followers to the Father's house so that they could be with Him forever (John 14:2-3). Promises made, promises kept! The supreme beauty of the eternal state is entering into an eternal rest in a perfect relationship with God.

With the eternal removal of sin, death, temptation, and evil, God eternally restores all that sin destroyed in the Garden of Eden. "And God shall wipe away all tears from their eyes; and there shall be no more death, neither sorrow, nor crying, neither shall there be any more pain: for the former things are passed away" (Rev. 21:4).

Sin ushered in weeping; God wipes it all away. Sin ushered in death; God conquers death forever and gives His eternal life. Sin ushered in sorrow, crying, and pain; God will abolish it all.

Then God speaks. "And he that sat upon the throne said, Behold, I make all things new. And he said unto me, Write: for these words are true and faithful" (Rev. 21:5). The Creator creates; the Word speaks.

Amazingly, God next spoke a word of invitation and warning for those still on this side of eternity.

Rise of the One-World Mind

And he said unto me, It is done. I am Alpha and Omega, the beginning and the end. I will give unto him that is athirst of the fountain of the water of life freely. He that overcometh shall inherit all things; and I will be his God, and he shall be my son. But the fearful, and unbelieving, and the abominable, and murderers, and whoremongers, and sorcerers, and idolaters, and all liars, shall have their part in the lake which burneth with fire and brimstone: which is the second death (Rev. 21:6-8).

If you are reading these words, you still have an opportunity to prepare for eternity. There are no other chances after you die. Jesus is offering you His free gift of eternal life. I urge you to receive it today before it is too late. Please do not go into the lake of fire. There is no need for you to die the second death since the offer of eternal life stands before you today.

In verse 9, John resumed his description of the New Jerusalem. Remember, there will be a new heaven and a new Earth. The description that follows in the remainder of Revelation 21 is not the totality of heaven but describes only the heavenly city called the New Jerusalem.

Interestingly, the number 12 plays a key role in the New Jerusalem.

- *12 gates with 12 angels (Rev. 21:12)*
- *12 gates bore the name of the 12 tribes of Israel (Rev. 21:12)*
- *12 foundations to the city which bore the names of the 12 apostles of the Lamb (21:14)*
- *The length, breadth, and height of the city is 12,000 furlongs in each direction (21:16).*
- *The wall is 144 cubits thick, which is 12 times 12 (Rev. 21:17)*
- *12 precious stones form the foundations of the wall (Rev. 21:19-20)*
- *12 gates were 12 pearls (Rev. 21:21)*
- *12 different fruits bore by the tree of life (Rev. 22:2)*

The New Jerusalem will be massive. 12,000 furlongs converts to about 1,500 miles, which is approximately the distance between New York City and Dallas, Texas. That puts the size of this city into perspective. Not only is it 1,500 miles in each direction, it is 1,500 miles tall.

Currently, the tallest building in the world is the Burj Khalifa in Dubai. It stands at an impressive 2,717 feet tall, which is just over half a mile tall. The highest peak in the world is Mount Everest, at approximately 5.5 miles above sea level. That means you would have to stack about 273 Mount Everests, or about 3,000 of the Burj Khalifa buildings on top of each other to reach the height of the New Jerusalem! Don't forget the walls of this New Jerusalem are over 200 feet thick.

John observed this enormous eternal city while standing on a "great and high mountain" (Rev. 21:10). If the city was this tall, how tall would the mountain be where John stood? The new heaven, new Earth, and New Jerusalem are going to blow our minds! A ministry colleague of ours would call it a Mindbender.

John returned the readers' focus to the central point of the New Jerusalem – Almighty God. "And I saw no temple therein: for the Lord God Almighty and the Lamb are the temple of it. And the city had no need of the sun, neither of the moon, to shine in it: for the glory of God did lighten it, and the Lamb is the light thereof" (Rev. 21:22-23).

The New Jerusalem serves as the throne of Almighty God. All His followers will enjoy an eternal relationship with Him.

> And he showed me a pure river of water of life, clear as crystal, proceeding out of the throne of God and of the Lamb. In the midst of the street of it, and on either side of the river, was there the tree of life, which bare twelve manner of fruits, and yielded her fruit every month: and the leaves of the tree were for the healing of the nations. And there shall be no more curse: but the throne of God and of the Lamb shall be in it; and his servants shall serve him: And they shall see his face; and his name shall be in their foreheads. And there shall be no night there; and they need no candle, neither light of the sun; for the Lord God giveth them light: and they shall reign for ever and ever (Rev. 22:1-5).

Jesus invites you to be in heaven with Him forever. After providing these details, this book of the Bible closes with one final invitation. "And the Spirit and the bride say, Come. And let him that heareth say, Come. And let him that is athirst come. And whosoever will, let him take the water of life freely" (Rev. 22:17).

For those who have trusted Jesus as their Savior, we must remember heaven. This wicked world drains our zeal. The daily onslaught of bad news threatens to discourage us. We must remember that our citizenship is in heaven.

Hebrews 11 is commonly called "The Hall of Faith" chapter of the Bible because it reminds us of how God used people when they walked with Him by faith. Faith calls us all to look to God despite the turmoil swirling around us in this world.

The author of Hebrews spoke of the patriarchs:

> These all died in faith, not having received the promises, but having seen them afar

off, and were persuaded of them, and embraced them, and confessed that they were
strangers and pilgrims on the earth. For they that say such things declare plainly that
they seek a country. And truly, if they had been mindful of that country from whence
they came out, they might have had opportunity to have returned. But now they desire
a better country, that is, an heavenly: wherefore God is not ashamed to be called their
God: for he hath prepared for them a city (Heb. 11:13-16).

They understood they were pilgrims in this world, and so should we. They had their eyes fixed and their hearts set on another country, and so should we. If they thought too much about where they came from, they might have turned back. Let this be a warning to us to remember the best is yet to come in the eternal heaven. They longed for that heavenly home, and so should we. They remembered the heavenly home that God had prepared for them, and so should we.

By the way, the word translated as "prepared" in Hebrews 11:16 is the same word Jesus used when He promised His disciples "I go to prepare a place for you" (John 14:2). When we remember heaven, we are ultimately remembering the promises of God for His people and the God who always keeps His promises.

There are many wonderful Christian songs about heaven. Some would argue, "Why should we write any more songs about heaven? There are too many as it is." I think this view is incorrect. Singing songs about heaven in church causes us to remember eternity and heaven. It encourages us to keep looking up with eyes of faith, as Hebrews 11:13-16 teaches. We can be reminded each Sunday that this world is not all there is. There is something far better just ahead for each follower of Jesus.

One such song was written in the 1950s by Southern Gospel singer and songwriter, Jim Hill (1930-2018), and is called "What a Day That Will Be."

> There is coming a day,
> When no heart aches shall come,
> No more clouds in the sky,
> No more tears to dim the eye,
> All is peace forevermore,
> On that happy golden shore,
> What a day, glorious day that will be.
> What a day that will be,
> When my Jesus I shall see,

And I look upon His face,
The One who saved me by His grace;
When He takes me by the hand,
And leads me through the Promised Land,
What a day, glorious day that will be.

There'll be no sorrow there,
No more burdens to bear,
No more sickness, no pain,
No more parting over there;
And forever I will be,
With the One who died for me,
What a day, glorious day that will be.

What a day that will be,
When my Jesus I shall see,
And I look upon His face,
The One who saved me by His grace;
When He takes me by the hand,
And leads me through the Promised Land,
What a day, glorious day that will be.

Reading those lyrics will minister to your soul and encourage you to remember the reality of heaven!

Remember Jesus

As this song reminds us, the greatest part of heaven is not "what," it is "who." The eternal state of the saved is only good because of God. Until we see Christ in eternity, we must keep our eyes firmly fixed upon Him every moment of every day.

When Jesus instituted the Lord's supper and informed His disciples that He was going to prepare a place for them, He called them to remember. As he broke the bread which symbolizes how His body would be broken on the cross, He instructed the disciples, "This do in remembrance of me" (Luke 22:19).

Churches today have "remembrance tables" that hold the bread and cup for observing the Lord's Supper. Many of these tables are inscribed with those words of Jesus. Worshippers are called to remember the sacrifice of Jesus on our behalf each time they partake of these elements. This powerful symbol reminds followers of who Jesus is and what He did for us.

After finishing the "Hall of Faith" chapter, the author of Hebrews wrote,

> *Wherefore seeing we also are compassed about with so great a cloud of witnesses, let us lay aside every weight, and the sin which doth so easily beset us, and let us run with patience the race that is set before us, Looking unto Jesus the author and finisher of our faith; who for the joy that was set before him endured the cross, despising the shame, and is set down at the right hand of the throne of God (Heb. 12:1-2).*

The "cloud of witnesses" the author refers to are all the followers of God who set an example of faith in Him. Christians are called to run this race of life like they did.

What if an Olympic runner lined up at the starting blocks while wearing a heavy backpack? They would be at an immediate disadvantage over the other runners since that backpack would slow down and tire out a runner well before the race is run.

So too sin inhibits the followers of Jesus from running this race of life to our full potential. We must cast it off through repentance so that we can run with endurance the race that is set before us, otherwise, we will face the mounting temptation to quit before the race is run.

While running this race, we must keep "looking unto Jesus." To say He is the "author and finisher of our faith" means that he is the trailblazer. He ran the race ahead of us. All we must do is follow in His footsteps by faith every step of the way until we reach the finish line.

Jesus endured the cross and won the greatest victory the world has ever witnessed as He defeated death, hell, and the grave! Christians do not run for victory but from victory. As Jesus cried from the cross, "It is finished" (John 19:30).

As we run this race and fight the good fight of faith, we must keep our eyes on Jesus. Toward the end of his race, the Apostle Paul wrote to Timothy, "I have fought a good fight, I have finished my course, I have kept the faith: Henceforth there is laid up for me a crown of righteousness, which the Lord, the righteous judge, shall give me at that day: and not to me only, but unto all them also that love his appearing" (2 Tim. 4:7-8).

At this juncture in my life, I think more about the finish line than the starting line. I want to finish well and "finish my course with joy, and the ministry, which I have received of the Lord Jesus, to testify the gospel of the grace of God." (Acts 20:24b).

The only way Paul could finish with such confidence was because He kept His eyes on Jesus. Nothing distracted him from running his course with joy. No sin held him back or caused him to quit running the race. May that be said of every follower of Jesus in our day!

I envision the true church today as a lighthouse. The world around us is enveloped in a dark and foreboding fog. People are in boats on the waves just hoping they can find their way safely to shore. The fog disorients and the waves constantly shift underneath them. Yet, the true church is firmly built upon the solid rock that is Jesus.

The true church must shine the light of Jesus into this present darkness. Prayerfully, those seeking safety will see the light and hasten to it. The church must be sure we do not allow sin to dim our light. How catastrophic it would be for others lost in the fog if we do!

Standing against the rise of the one-world mind can distract us if we are not vigilant to keep our eyes on Jesus. As I noted from the outset, I have not shared the truths of this book to scare you but to help you open your eyes to the reality of what is happening in the world today.

It's one thing to open our eyes, it's another thing to know where to look once our eyes are open. If we look only at the one-world headlines, we will stay off course. If our only response is to build a bunker and fill it with supplies, we will stay off course.

Here's a temptation unique to students of Bible prophecy. If our study of end-times events is filled more with the Antichrist than Jesus Christ, we have missed the whole point of Bible prophecy. The first words in the book of Revelation are, "The Revelation of Jesus Christ" (Rev. 1:1). This book of the Bible is not primarily the revelation of end-times events. It is not primarily the revelation of the unholy trinity. It is first and foremost the revelation of Jesus Christ!

This is why I have spent the last chapters of this book developing a roadmap for you to walk with the Lord in these last days. This is why I am ending this book by pointing you to Jesus, the trailblazer of our faith.

Yes, the one-world system will come. Yes, the Antichrist will rule during the end times. Daniel 7:21 says, "I beheld, and the same horn made war with the saints, and prevailed against them." This is a reference to the Antichrist defeating those who will be saved during the Great Tribulation. Many of these tribulation saints will die as martyrs when they refuse to follow the Antichrist's global system of worship, government, and economy (Rev. 7:9-17, 13:15).

Yes, the Antichrist rises, but do not miss the next verse in Daniel 7. "Until the Ancient of days came, and judgment was given to the saints of the most High; and the time came that the saints possessed the kingdom" (Dan. 7:22).

Jesus wins! He will put down the Antichrist for all eternity at the Second Coming just before the Millennial Reign of Christ on Earth commences. John described this victorious scene in Revelation 19.

> And I saw heaven opened, and behold a white horse; and he that sat upon him was called Faithful and True, and in righteousness he doth judge and make war. His eyes were as a flame of fire, and on his head were many crowns; and he had a name written, that no man knew, but he himself. And he was clothed with a vesture dipped in blood: and his name is called The Word of God. And the armies which were in heaven followed him upon white horses, clothed in fine linen, white and clean. And out of his mouth goeth a sharp sword, that with it he should smite the nations: and he shall rule them with a rod of iron: and he treadeth the winepress of the fierceness and wrath of Almighty God. And he hath on his vesture and on his thigh a name written, KING OF KINGS, AND LORD OF LORDS.

> And I saw an angel standing in the sun; and he cried with a loud voice, saying to all the fowls that fly in the midst of heaven, Come and gather yourselves together unto the supper of the great God; That ye may eat the flesh of kings, and the flesh of captains, and the flesh of mighty men, and the flesh of horses, and of them that sit on them, and the flesh of all men, both free and bond, both small and great.

> And I saw the beast, and the kings of the earth, and their armies, gathered together to make war against him that sat on the horse, and against his army. And the beast was taken, and with him the false prophet that wrought miracles before him, with which he deceived them that had received the mark of the beast, and them that worshipped his image. These both were cast alive into a lake of fire burning with brimstone. And the remnant were slain with the sword of him that sat upon the horse, which sword proceeded out of his mouth: and all the fowls were filled with their flesh (Rev. 19:11-21).

The Conquering King returns to Earth with His saints and establishes His Millennial Kingdom. I am on the winning side through faith in Jesus Christ; I hope you are too.

When Jesus informed and warned His disciples about what would come during the end times, He gave them this encouragement, "And when these things begin to come to pass, then look up, and lift up your heads; for your redemption draweth nigh" (Luke 21:28).

This is not the time for followers of Jesus to hang their heads and hide. We don't have to fearfully peek through closed blinds. If anyone in this world ought to be happy, grateful, and joyful, it is the true church. Our greatest moments are just ahead! Since Jesus is our Savior, the victory is already ours. Go forward in faith in the face of the rising one-world system. "Look up, and lift up your heads; for your redemption draweth nigh."